Endors

Faith is the currency of the supernatural. This book will equip you to enter the next phase of God's Spirit—mountain-moving faith!

SID ROTH
Host, *It's Supernatural!*

One of the most important and frequently overlooked elements of the end-times renewal is its rediscovery of the ministry of healing, both for the body of Christ and in evangelism. I am greatly encouraged that so many Christians are writing about the ministry of healing and motivating the entire body of Christ to practice it. In *Command Your Healing,* Dr. Hakeem Collins has written a book that focuses on key elements in the ministry of healing, specifically the relationship between healing, faith, and your words. When these three elements are properly employed, as they were in the ministry of Jesus, we too can see the healing power of God released around the world. I recommend that you study this book and apply its insights in your ministry to the sick.

JOAN HUNTER, Evangelist
Author of *Healing Starts Now*
Joan Hunter Ministries
www.joanhunter.org

In this book, *Command Your Healing,* Dr. Hakeem Collins masterfully walks readers through the principles and power of divine healing as found in Scripture. He extrapolates from Bible stories and real-life anecdotes in order to empower believers to *Command Their Healing.* Even those who don't believe that healing is for today, after finishing this insightful read they will be persuaded that divine healing *is* for today. Just as God speaks in many different ways, He also heals in many ways in response to our faith and standing on His Word. I highly recommend this dynamic literary work for new and seasoned believers alike. You will not be disappointed; you will receive faith for your appointed healing commanded by Heaven!

APOSTLE DEMONTAE EDMONDS
Freedom 4 the Nations
Covenant Connections Ministry Alliance
www.f4nations.com
Virginia Beach, Virginia

This book is a mindful masterpiece about the miracle of healing. A must-read for anyone looking to share or experience the healing power of our heavenly Father. The daily devotional is a practical guide to silencing deadly fears and turning up the volume on the life-giving Word of God. Dr. Collins taps into the heart of God and pours out His healing virtue on all who read these pages.

EFREM GRAHAM
CBN News Anchor and Correspondent

In Genesis 1, we see a pattern. God spoke after the Spirit fell. There was power when the word was spoken through the Holy Spirit. This simple, fundamental truth is made evident in Dr. Hakeem Collins' new book, *Command Your Healing*. No longer does a believer have to struggle with a spirit of infirmity or weak prayers. Through the powerful insights and direction contained within these pages, you can take authority over every affliction and struggle. Learn how to speak through the power and anointing of the Holy Spirit and see, feel, and testify to the greatness of God and the power of the spoken word. Your healing is at your command!

RABBI ERIC E. WALKER
Executive Director/On-Air
Host of *Revealing the Truth*
Igniting a Nation, Inc.

Dr. Hakeem Collins is a well-educated, passionate, and authoritative person taking what he knows in the natural and mixing it with his prophetic voice and insights. His love for Jesus and those intimate moments he shares with Him allow Dr. Collins to bring you supernatural insights combined with scriptural revelation to leave you empowered and equipped to call forth and manifest your healing. Dr. Collins does not only write, but also lives and implements the very word He preaches. You will be blessed and empowered to walk in the full manifestation of the healing power Jesus purchased for you through reading the truths in this book, *Command Your Healing*.

KATHY DEGRAW
Founder, DeGraw Ministries and Be Love Outreach
Author of *Speak Out*
www.degrawministries.org

Command Your Healing is a timely and much needed Kingdom resource that speaks to the reality of life's issues and the remedy to those same issues. Dr. Hakeem Collins' book provides practical biblical principles of positive thinking, speaking, and acting that causes you to tap into the realm of consistent, supernatural success and the healing breakthrough you are believing God for. *Command Your Healing* is a good read that presents powerful information in a unique way. This book causes you to identify the "success enemies" in your life and gives you a practical plan of action to overcome those enemies with time-tested, biblical laws and principles that always work—if you work them!

REVEREND ERIC WILLIAMS
Good Word Ministries
Trenton, New Jersey

I'm excited for Dr. Hakeem Collins' newest book, *Command Your Healing*. This is an invaluable resource for all who want to receive their healing and also those who want to be used to operate in the gift of healing. I believe the release of this book is the prophetic timing of the Lord! In an hour when so many people are suffering with pain and sickness, God is raising up an army of warriors who will carry His healing anointing to the nations. Healing is a vital part of our spiritual inheritance in Christ and a key component to living out the ministry of Jesus today. Jesus not only preached the good news, He revealed the Father's goodness through healing the sick and setting the oppressed free!

Through this book, Dr. Hakeem Collins reveals scriptural truths and testimonies from his own life and ministry that will grow your faith so you can access the healing power that is already yours through the finished work of the cross. Also, the 90-day devotional and faith confessions included in the book teach how to practically and supernaturally release healing into your own body as well as those around you who are desperately in need of His healing touch. This book will not only encourage you, it will catapult you into a greater realm of healing power that you never imagined possible for you!

MICHAEL LOMBARDO, International Minister
Author, *Immersed in His Glory*
President and Founder of Life Poured Out International
www.lifepouredoutintl.org

Command Your Healing is one of the most powerfully written healing devotional books I have ever read. As you read each chapter, there is such a raw anointing of healing being released. Dr. Hakeem Collins masterfully recaptures believers' authority to see Jesus' supernatural ministry of healing being exercised and released in their lives. This is a uniquely written 90-day devotional book that will literally activate healing in the lives of every reader with prayers, commands, and confessions of faith that will release the power of healing.

This highly recommended book is loaded with personal testimonies and stories of God's miraculous power of Dr. Hakeem learning and sharing secrets to activating healing, signs, wonders, and miracles through the authority of commanding. You will learn how to move from the realm of praying by faith to commanding by faith. Both King David in the Old Testament and Jesus Christ in the New Testament revealed the incredible power of *Commanding Your Healing* outlined in Psalm 107:20 and in Matthew 8:7-8 respectively. Interestedly, in both passages of Scripture, you will very easily see a position of authority exercised where the acts of healing did not necessarily come by praying but by commanding. *Command Your Healing* intentionally puts the authority back into the life of the Spirit-filled believer to prophesy and decree healing that carries rank not just as a believer in healing but a *commander* in healing.

DR. NAIM COLLINS, President

Fan the Flames Global Ministries, Naim Collins Ministries
www.naimcollinsministries.com

Command Your Healing is a thought-provoking and profound read. It takes readers into an amazing journey into the authority and identity of who they are in Christ. Dr. Hakeem Collins gives powerful principles that help us unlock our divine healing and teaches us how to remain healed. This is a treasure truly for the masses. I recommend this book for inclusion in every church curriculum.

Prophet SHAWN MORRIS
Author, *How to TAP in the Glory of God*

COMMAND

your

Healing

OTHER BOOKS BY DR. HAKEEM COLLINS

Prophetic Breakthrough

Heaven Declares: Prophetic Decrees to Start Your Day

Born to Prophesy: God's Voice Speaking Through You

COMMAND
your
Healing

PROPHETIC DECLARATIONS TO
RECEIVE AND RELEASE HEALING POWER

HAKEEM COLLINS

Disclaimer: This book, *Command Your Healing*, is not intended to be a substitute or replacement for the medical attention, advice, or directives of your physicians. The reader should regularly consult a physician in matters relating to his or her health condition, and particularly with respect to any symptoms that may require diagnosis or immediate medical attention. The information contained in this book is designed to provide helpful information on the subjects discussed. *Command Your Healing* book is not meant to be used, nor should it be used, to treat, diagnose any medical conditions. For diagnosis or medical treatment of any medical issue, problem, or complications, we advise you seek your own physician. In the case of an emergency please call 911. Please be advised that the *publisher* and *author* of this book, *Command Your Healing*, are not held responsible for any specific health or allergy needs that may require direct medical supervision, and are not liable for any damages or negative consequences for any treatment, action, application, or preparation to any individuals or person(s) reading or following the information provided in this book.

Biblical and scriptural references are for informational purposes only, and do not constitute endorsement of any websites or other sources. Various names and identifying details have been changed to protect the privacy of individuals; although some personal testimonies have been cited with permission. Readers should be aware that the websites listed in this book may change.

DESTINY IMAGE® PUBLISHERS, INC.

P.O. Box 310, Shippensburg, PA 17257-0310

"Promoting Inspired Lives."

This book and all other Destiny Image and Destiny Image Fiction books are available at Christian bookstores and distributors worldwide.

Cover design by Eileen Rockwell

Interior design by Terry Clifton

For more information on foreign distributors, call 717-532-3040.

Or reach us on the Internet: www.destinyimage.com

ISBN 13 TP: 978-0-7684-4279-3
ISBN 13 F.Book: 978-0-7684-4280-9
ISBN HC: 978-0-7684-4282-3
ISBN LP: 978-0-7684-4281-6

For Worldwide Distribution, Printed in the U.S.A.

1 2 3 4 5 6 / 21 20 19 18

Contents

PART ONE

COMMAND

Your

Healing

CHAPTER 1

Healing Breakthrough

When evening had come, they brought to Him many who were demon-possessed. And He cast out the spirits with a word, and healed all who were sick, that it might be fulfilled which was spoken by Isaiah the prophet, saying: "He Himself took our infirmities and bore our sicknesses" (Matthew 8:16-17).

*C*ommand Your Healing is a teaching on healing and a 90-day devotional that reveals the heartbeat of God concerning healing and miracles that you can receive through faith. The Father desires His people to come into present-truth reformation on healing in the Scriptures. Faith is the doorway to your healing breakthrough. The faith confessions and commands contained in this book will motivate you each day to drown out the negative reports of sickness and shatter the thought of owning it.

Whether you are in dire need of a healing breakthrough, or you may know someone who needs the healing power of God, I have written this book to increase your faith in Jesus and the healing anointing available here and now. I always say that *faith will dismantle the fear in the supernatural healing power of God.*

What is limiting you from receiving your healing? What report from the doctor has discouraged you from believing God can change the report? What generational sickness or disease is blocking you from receiving your total healing victory? What lie of the enemy is causing you to believe that healing is not for today? Or what false teaching on present-day healing were you exposed to that says healing, miracles, prophecies, and the gifts of the Holy Spirit are not operative today that has caused you to lose faith and hope in God's supernatural power? If you purchased this book or were given this book, then faith is the premise for you to receive your healing breakthrough today.

I wholeheartedly believe that today is the first day of your healing breakthrough. As you read chapter by chapter and go through the healing commands and prophetic faith confessions, you will begin to see your faith increase to another level. Your faith will start the healing process on the road to recovery!

FAITH COMES

The Bible says, *"faith comes by hearing, and hearing by the word of God"* (Romans 10:17). Let me put it like this in regard to receiving your healing breakthrough in my own words: *"Faith comes by hearing, and hearing by your healing faith expectations in God's Word."* As Christian believers, we must *believe* in what the Word of God says about healing. The Word of God is truth, and we must accept it to be just that. God cannot lie because He is absolute truth (see Num. 23:19)

As Spirit-filled believers, we possess words of life in our tongues as we declare, decree, confess, and command God's Word with Holy Spirit boldness and authority. Jesus says in John 6:63, *"It is the Spirit who gives life; the flesh profits nothing. The words that I speak to you are spirit, and they are life."* Jesus' life-giving words contain the breath of life that brings total healing and wholeness. We must confess with our mouths what we want to see happen in our lives. Faith has ears and we must give the Word of God a voice! Fuel your faith with healing confessions and commands that will bring about the best results you are supernaturally believing and expecting.

Out of the abundance of the heart, the mouth speaks (see Luke 6:45). Fill your days with healing Scriptures, prayers, confessions, and prophetic words from the heart of God that will heal, inspire, motivate, strengthen, empower, revive, and transform you.

Each daily entry found within Part Two of this book is loaded with power-packed, faith-inspiring, and invoking words of life from the Father that will cause your current condition to take a sudden turn for the best. God wants to turn your present situation into a divine solution. Sickness and disease is not your portion!

Unfortunately, there are believers today walking around wearing spiritual blinders, not knowing their spiritual authority in Christ. They must know without a shadow of doubt that they are called to be made whole. As Christian believers, we must arm ourselves with the Word of God so that we can combat and disarm all demonic curses, sickness, and diseases that brings discomfort—mentally and physically.

Isaiah 54:17 (NASB) says:

"No weapon that is formed against you will prosper; and every tongue that accuses you in judgment you will condemn. This is the heritage of the servants of the Lord, and their vindication is from Me," declares the Lord.

LIFE IN THE POWER OF THE TONGUE

As Christian believers, we are not to sit on the sidelines of life and allow sickness, disease, the spirit of infirmities, curses, and poverty to take control or dictate our lives. We can see from the passage of Scripture in Isaiah 54:17 that the weapon was formed, but will not succeed. Every day the enemy has an arsenal of weaponry with your name on it. It is imperative to know that you are on the devil's hit list. It is the enemy's design and desire for you to walk in ignorance, so that he can take full of advantage of the opportunity.

But, I believe we have the prophetic advantage and supernatural edge and strategy by truth in God's Word to combat and counteract any hit the devil wants to launch. Heaven is declaring what God is intending for *you* to possess and inherit by the Holy Spirit. The Bible says that there is *"death and life in the power of the tongue"* (Proverbs 18:21). We can resurrect things by the very words we speak, or we can crucify things in like manner. God has given us a powerful instrument in our mouths—called the tongue. We have the ability to speak prophetically with creativity through the power of our words.

Did you know that you have the authority to permit and prohibit things from happening in your life through your words? I am not talking about naming and claiming anything and everything you want in the name of Jesus. I am referring to knowing the truths of God's Word and speaking them forth in faith in your life. I want to be very clear that I am not a proponent of the naming and claiming theology or teaching. This is not the premise of this book or purpose of confessing and commanding prophetically for healing—it is all about knowing your spiritual authority, legal rights and benefits as a child of God.

I am talking about speaking, declaring what God says, and obtaining them through His Word in acts of obedience. Obedience and believing in God's Word is key to accessing what God says you can access. I am referring to knowing your God-given ability and authority as a child of God to bind and loose things, to speak words of life, healing, encouragement, and edification.

Do you realize that you do not have to allow sickness and disease to plague your life and the lives of those you love? You have the power in Jesus' name to command healing by your confessions of the Word of God.

One of the aspects that stands out to me in regard to Jesus' authority in His earthly ministry is that He *commanded* things to happen concerning healing and deliverance from demon spirits.

What are the things in your life that you are allowing to exist? What sickness, disease, illness, or pain has taken residence in your body? This is the time to take up your bed and walk. In other words, take up your authority and live again.

Furthermore, Jesus *commanded* His disciples (apostles) to heal the sick, drive out demon spirits, cure diseases, and preach the Kingdom of God (see Matthew 10:1; Luke 9:1, 10:1). Jesus commanded with authority, never doubting, second-guessing, or assuming; as a result, healing and miracles manifested by what He spoke. Faith in God's Word and believing the spoken words that we speak of healing will happen in our lives. We can command our healing in Jesus' name and walk in the authority, power, and grace of His name as believers. Not only the word *command* was a direct order, but also it was a principle that the Spirit of God can demonstrate.

COMMANDING YOUR HEALING

Webster's New World Dictionary defines the word *command* as, "to give an order to, direct, to have authority over, control, to have for use, controlling power or position, and mastery." In other words, as Christian, Spirit-filled believers, we must understand that even by the definition we are to give a direct order over sickness, disease, and illness to vacate and exit. God has given His people controlling power through the Holy Spirit to master anything that is not like Him in our lives, that are operating illegally in our body. Whatever we have given legal ground to—for sickness or disease or curses to exist—we must repent, renounce, and give up the legal right for them to exist.

Moreover, you must understand that you have controlling and commanding authority by the Holy Spirit to take control of your life, mind, body, and soul. Know your position and legal, biblical rights in the Kingdom to fight back against evil, unrighteousness, and sicknesses. The Commander and Chief Jesus Christ has given you delegated commands to overcome the plans of the enemy. The Father has given you a direct order to not only heal others but that you can command *your own* healing by speaking the prophetic confessions and commands of faith.

Jesus did not give an order or command to His disciples; He delegated His authority to them. He told (commanded) His disciples to heal the sick because He knew they could be healed. Furthermore, we can see that Jesus never instructed His disciples to pray for the sick but commanded them to *heal* the sick. I believe it is not just for those who are in healing ministries to heal the sick, but all Spirit-filled believers are also commanded to speak healing over themselves. In other words, we have the power to bring healing to ourselves.

Self-healing is something I believe can happen supernaturally by faith in God's Word, because it happened to me when my jaw was broken by an unexpected assault. There have been many times in a healing service when I would give testimony of a miracle that had taken place, and those in attendance would receive their healing breakthrough just by the spoken word of testimony of healing. There is overcoming healing power that comes by healing testimonies.

The enemy comes to steal, kill, and destroy; but Jesus comes that we might have life and have it more abundantly (see John 10:10). It is the devil's desire to delay and deny us of our full healing breakthrough by bringing fear and unbelief in the finished work of the cross. We can overcome the adversary by the blood of the Lamb and by the word of our testimony (see Revelation 12:11). There is something powerful in the Word of God and the word of our testimony. Healing testimonies can release corporate healing to multitudes of people at one time.

Hearing about healing and breakthroughs that God has done for someone can increase our faith to receive it for ourselves without anyone laying their hands on us. I believe that *words of healing testimonies unleash Holy Spirit power and can activate the supernatural.* I will tell you about what God did for me supernaturally later on in this book. We have the authority to speak or command healing to occur in our lives and in the lives of others in need. That is why I called this healing devotional and teaching, *Command Your Healing.* We can receive our own healing in Jesus' name. Remember, Jesus declared that believers could do the same works that He did while on earth, and He went on to say that believers could do greater works than He did.

> *I tell you the truth, anyone who believes in me will do the same works I have done, and even greater works, because I am going to be with the Father. You can ask for anything in my name, and I will do it, so that the Son can bring glory to the Father. 14 Yes, ask me for anything in my name, and I will do it!* (John 14:12-14 NLT)

As we know, Jesus is God in the flesh and possessed unlimited power; but as a man on earth, He was bound by human limitations. The truth in the passage from John 14 is that those who believe on Jesus and the supernatural works of the Father will do them—and even greater works than what Jesus demonstrated.

I believe today, in the twenty-first century, we are seeing the greater works ministry of the Holy Spirit being unleashed in qualitative ways. We are in the days of glory, which signify the unprecedented moves of God's Spirit releasing unusual miracles in the life of believers in rapid succession. The God of miracles is performing creative miracles and healing around the world through those possessing radical faith to believe Him for them. Faith is being activated to cause Heaven to come to earth through the prophetic words released from the throne room of God.

We are in the days of the "greater works outpouring" of God's Spirit upon all flesh. They will not only prophesy, have visions, and be dreamers of dreams, but the healing working power of God is being displayed as well, since Pentecost (read Joel 2:28-29; Acts 2:1-4). Let us look at something that I believe will bless you and revolutionize your paradigm when it comes to the truth of God's Word concerning healing. I want to break every lie by some Bible cessationist teachers, and those who are the proponents of healing ministries, word of faith teachers, modern-day prophets and apostles and the like, who say that God is not performing miracles and healing today.

Let us look at what the word "command" means in the context of Scripture and what I believe is essential to know when it pertains to you receiving your healing breakthrough here and now. I believe in miracles, healing, and especially you receiving yours today, which is why I wrote this book. In John chapter 14 verse 12, the context is self-explanatory—that believer can do what Jesus did and greater works as well. But when we go on to verses 13 and 14, the meaning takes a different turn and is not as self-explanatory or evident and needs more definitive understanding.

COMMAND ANYTHING IN JESUS' NAME

And whatever you ask in My name, that I will do, that the Father may be glorified in the Son. If you ask anything in My name, I will do it (John 14:13-14).

I want you to pay a close attention to the word "ask" in verses 13 and 14. These two words are very important and we can see that they are used twice. The word "ask" here in these verses is the Greek word *aiteo,* which means to "ask, beg, call for, crave, desire and to require" in the strongest manner and expression possible when it refers and applies to people (Strong's

Concordance G154). The word *aiteo* more frequently suggests the attitude of a suppliant, the petition of one who is lesser in position than the person to whom the petition is made. For example, as Christian believers we are asking God for something as His children (see Matthew 7:7).

My question to you: Is healing a "whatever" or an "anything?" The word "ask" also means "to command" when used on a "whatever" or "anything." We can see that healing is a "whatever" or "anything." In other words, as believers we do not ask a thing or a whatever, but we can *command* it! Jesus did not tell His disciples to *pray* for healing but to *command* healing to happen. However, we know that praying for the sick is biblical; but the emphasis here and primarily throughout the New Testament is the disciples and apostles asked by the act of commanding verbally healing to happen. They moved in a realm of expectation by faith. When Jesus gives His people authority to heal the sick, raise the dead and so much more, it was a command that needed to be carried out. If Jesus commanded His disciples to heal the sick, then by His command they are ordered and able to heal in His name.

This is a biblical principle that must be embraced. For example, if someone gives you authority to do something, you do not have to second-guess it. Why? Because you have been given the rights by the person authorized. For example, if I give you access to unlock my car, you must have the keys given to you by the owner, me, and my permission to use them. You do not have to question yourself or second-guess if I have given you keys to access my car, because it is my vehicle and I have given you full access and authority to enter.

Likewise, the Sender, being Jesus Christ, has given us, as Spirit-filled believers, full access to the power of His Word. Jesus is the One authorized to give His people the authority to heal others, and even themselves, by the Holy Spirit. You do not have to question the authority released to you by Jesus through the Holy Spirit.

There was a Nike commercial I liked when I used to play collegiate football. The brand slogan and motto was *"Just do it!"* I believe the Lord is saying to His people, *"Just do it by faith!"* Or, *"Just heal the sick"* by faith. Know that if Jesus has given His people delegated authority and permission to do something, then He knows without a shadow of doubt that it can be done—because He Himself has done it. This same principle can be applied for personal healing, miracles, and breakthrough. You can *command* your own healing. You can speak it by faith through the principle and authority given by God's Word. Whatever or anything that you may be faced with, just rest assured that your situation, circumstance, and condition has to obey and bow to the name of Jesus Christ.

This is a key principle in receiving healing. Healing is in fact a "whatever" and an "anything." We can see this with apostle Peter in reference to asking whatever and anything in Jesus' name shared in verses 13 and 14 in John chapter 14, that he knew he could do what Jesus did and greater. Peter also knew the revelation that Jesus could simply speak to sickness and they who heard the words of healing were all healed. In other words, Jesus can simply command by speaking to sickness and disease, and He must be obeyed. The apostle Peter could do the same as Jesus and so can *you*. We can command healing to happen in Jesus' name, and it will be done to bring glory to the Father. We have to put "whatever and anything" that is contrary to healing in its place in Jesus' name.

TAKE UP YOUR BED AND WALK!

"So I will prove to you that the Son of Man has the authority on earth to forgive sins." Then Jesus turned to the paralyzed man and said, "Stand up, pick up your mat, and go home!" And the man jumped up and went home! Fear swept through the crowd as they saw this happen. And they praised God for giving humans such authority (Matthew 9:6-8 NLT).

In the passage in Matthew 9, Jesus used a different Greek word in regard to "asking." Jesus used a much more toned-down Greek word *lego*, which is a regular word for "speak" or "say." The word "say" is a milder tone and not as strong as the word "command." We have to understand that there is power in the name of Jesus. Jesus did not command (*aiteo*) in Matthew 9:6-8, He simply spoke (*lego*) to the man with the palsy by saying to him to arise and the man arose and departed the house.

Jesus can heal just by simply "saying." Peter used the similar word "say" (*lego*) to heal a person with palsy. He used a stronger expression by commanding (*aiteo*) for the palsy man to arise. The Greek word *lego* means, "to say, to speak, affirm over, maintain, advise, direct and to command" (Strong's G3004). Jesus, when He is speaking healing to someone, is basically commanding directly to a person to be healed. Jesus is using a stronger tone and giving directives or an order for something to happen. If He was casting out demon spirits, He still used the word *lego,* but it was an intense direct command (*aiteo*).

My point is that Peter commanded healing, in a "whatever" or in an "any kind of thing" situation. Peter needed raw courage and boldness to speak and command healing for someone. Maybe you do not possess this kind of faith right now—but I believe that you will after reading this book. You will be like Peter and command your healing. It will take Holy-Spirit boldness, faith, and courage to declare what your outcome and results will be.

One of the problems is the lack of faith to believe God to do the miraculous in our lives. We have to believe that whatever situation or condition we find ourselves in, that we can command a different outcome and result by the Holy Spirit's authority and power. Have you found yourself praying for healing and nothing happened? Have you ever found yourself praying the Word of God and saw no or few results?

I believe it's our faith to act and confess with authority what we are speaking that will produce results. I believe we must command our healing daily. I believe that God wants His people to have mountain-moving faith, to command by speaking to whatever and any situation that is unmovable, like a mountain, and command it to move. We have to become risk takers by faith in the Spirit and operate in the raw type of faith that Peter possessed to see results of healing and miracles. Things may seem impossible, but the impossible is possible in Christ.

SPEAK TO YOUR MOUNTAIN CONDITION!

Mark 11:23-24 says:

For assuredly, I say to you, whoever, says to this mountain, "Be removed and be cast into the sea," and does not doubt in his heart, but believes that those things he says will be done, he will have whatever he says. Therefore I say to you, whatever things you ask when you pray, believe that you receive them, and you will have them (Mark 11:23-2).

What a profound and faith-invoking Scripture! Mark 11:23-24 says that we can simply say or speak to any mountain in our lives and command it to move—and it will be removed. We must understand that as Spirit-filled believers we can speak directly to the mountain (sickness, disease) and command it to leave by faith in our heart, knowing that with our authority in Christ and the power of His name we can command (*aiteo*) and speak (*lego*) things to happen.

Interestingly, the word for "say" in Mark 11:23 is the Greek word *epos,* which means to speak, say, and goes on to mean "command, grant and tell" (Strong's G2031). In verse 23 we see the word "say" three times, which gives slightly the same meaning. Jesus says (*lego*) to His disciples through a direct command, that whoever speaks (*epos*) to this mountain to be removed, cast into the sea, and does not doubt in their heart, but shall believe, that those things that they say through a command, direct order, or calling out by name will be done.

What specific illness, sickness, pain, or whatever is refusing to be removed from your life? We have to command by saying or speaking prophetically to every specific mountainous situation, and order it to leave us for good. For example, if you were to speak to someone specifically in a crowd of people, you would have to call out that person's name directly to pin point the particular person. Sickness, illness, infirmities, and disease have names and we can speak by commanding them directly to leave us by calling them out by name.

Prophesy through speaking has the power to bring forth and also call out from. We are to speak to mountains and they will listen and respond to the direct order. Remember that it is not a prayer that will move mountains, as Jesus never prayed for the sick. Jesus spoke to the sick and diseased. I am

13

not saying that we are not to pray for the sick or pray for God to intervene on the behalf of someone or healing for ourselves. My point is that we must take hold of what we possess by the Holy Spirit and speak prophetic healing and the Father's results of a good report or news over ourselves. We have to use the power of the spoken words to see mountains moved and relocated in Jesus' name.

Oftentimes, Jesus commanded by speaking healing directly and firmly to those who were ill, sick, diseased, and crippled. We have to establish a template of healing speech in our minds so that when we are decreeing and commanding our own healing, we own it through and in the name of Jesus! We can command through the eyes of faith—whatever part of our bodies that need healing or a miracle.

WORDS OF COMMAND

The word "command" is very powerful and direct. We are not asking God to heal us; we know by His command that we *can* be healed and by faith in His Word that we *are* healed. We, as faith believers, have to command our opposing situations and circumstances to change—or there will be no change. Did you know that sickness, disease, and the like have ears? This might sound strange, but it is true. When Jesus would work a miracle or heal someone, He spoke a word of command to the sickness and the disease, not to the person *per se*. In other words, if someone is plagued by cancer, you have to speak directly and firmly to the cancer itself, not the person. The person's body became the host of the disease.

Following are a few biblical examples that illustrate and explain my point of Jesus commanding healing to take place. One example is when Jesus heals the sick man at the pool of Bethesda. He commanded the man to *"Rise, take up your bed and walk"* (John 5:8).

In Matthew 12:13, Jesus commanded the man with the withered hand to *"Stretch out your hand,"* and when the man obeys the command of Jesus, his hand was restored completely. Moreover, Jesus' apostles and disciples followed His healing model, teaching and speaking healing commands, as described in Acts 3:6, with the healing of a crippled man: *"Then Peter said,*

'Silver and gold I do not have, but what I do have I give to you: In the name of Jesus Christ of Nazareth, rise up and walk.'" In the next verse, Peter took the lame man by the right hand and lifted him up on his feet, and immediately his feet and ankle bones received supernatural strength (Acts 3:7).

What are the healing commands that you desire to speak over yourself and see happen? Is it unbelief, doubt, or your current condition that is causing you to be numb to the biblical fact and truth that God wants you, or whoever you are believing God for, to be totally healed? Hebrews 13:8 declares that *"Jesus is the same yesterday, today, and forever."* Jesus is the same always, and His view on seeing you healed hasn't changed either. Jesus can heal you from sickness yesterday, and can do the same today for you if you need Him to, and tomorrow if you have an issue plaguing you. His method of healing you may change, but the healing results are the same. God the Father desires to see you walk in your divine health, and that brings Him glory.

The glory of God is released when we embrace what Heaven is declaring for us to possess. Have you ever been in a place where you were standing in need of a personal miracle? Were you ever in dire need of a divine intervention from Heaven? Has there ever been a time in your life when you have asked others to pray by standing in the gap for you by touching and agreeing for a healing breakthrough? Whether you needed a healing physically, emotionally, or psychologically, it's nothing like being the one in need of God performing a miracle in your life. Heaven is listening to the cries of His people, especially those who are in desperate need of a healing, miracle, deliverance, and breakthrough.

CHAPTER 2

Words of Healing

"Lord, help!" they cried in their trouble, and he saved them from their distress. He sent out his word and healed them, snatching them from the door of death. Let them praise the Lord for his great love and for the wonderful things he has done for them (Psalm 107:19-21 NLT).

Notice that the Father is willing and more than able to assist those who call upon Him in time of trouble. He will relieve them of their distress by sending His Word to heal and to deliver them from all destructions. Oftentimes, there are things that happen in our lives that catch us off guard and take us by surprise. Normally, we would rather live our lives uninterrupted, but we know that is impossible in today's world while living for Christ. Crises at times cannot be avoided. We need Christ in times of crisis! God will give His children direction by the Holy Spirit to navigate life by ordering our steps daily to keep us out of harm's way.

Life in general has the potential to make us or break us. There are individuals daily facing all types of life-altering situations, circumstances that cause them to make crucial decisions that may be life or death. I was faced with a situation in my own family when a person's fate was in our hands. In other words, the person's life expectancy was no longer a personal decision of theirs, but was up to the family to decide. Can you imagine someone else determining your life expectancy; you have no say or control over what is decided? Can you imagine someone thinking for you by assuming that you would rather transition to meet the Father than to be healed by Him to live and not die?

There are tremendous burdens to undertake when you have a family member who is on life support and in a coma. The person's life is literally at the mercy of your decision as to whether or not to "pull the plug." For the family or family member making that hard decision, there are many factors to consider, including not knowing if the person will ever make it out of a coma or if the person even knows what state of consciousness he or she is experiencing. Deciding whether someone lives or dies is the hardest decision to make.

As a Christian believer, the best interest in my mind at the time my family and I were in that situation was for God's will to be done and allow God to be God. His will is for the person to live. It was my advice for the family to allow God to make that determination to welcome my Aunt Pauline home to Heaven or to allow her to finish out her race on the earth.

It is an even harder decision to make when the situation is unclear and the doctors say there is nothing more they can do. What do we do then? We have to turn to the Lord. These types of situations require the wisdom and counsel of the Lord. The family member I am referring to was actually my cousin, but I called my great aunt. She was in a coma due to a life-long illness, and the family had to make an imminent decision due to financial burdens and obligations that her hospital stay created, and because the doctors couldn't do anything else for her. She was in her late 70s and the likelihood of coming out of the coma was very slim. So her children were faced with a big decision to make—whether Aunt Pauline would live on earth or transition to Heaven.

BELIEVER OF FAITH

I loved my dear great aunt who was a strong woman of faith. Beginning at the age of 7, I watched her in the Baptist church serving the Lord with all of her heart. She was considered a matriarch in the Baptist church I attended as a child. She always wore beautiful and classy clothes and large, matching hats. She was a straightforward and vocal woman who always spoke her mind, but with the love of the Lord. Aunt Pauline was what I called one of the "church mothers." A church mother was a seasoned, praying woman who would gather the young women to impart wisdom about how to conduct themselves in church as ladies. My aunt possessed the gift of discerning of spirits and was able to discern if someone was not living according to biblical principles, values, and standards. My great aunt Pauline was the standard barrier and model for young women to follow after.

Moreover, I always had strong women in my life, like my mother Paula Collins, my godmother (who is actually my cousin) Zakiya Minkah, and grandmother Ruth Collins who introduced me to Jesus through my church, Union Baptist Church in Wilmington, Delaware. These women were examples and heroes of faith. When my great aunt was hospitalized, I knew at that time that God was going to show me something prophetic and sovereign. When we received the call that she fell into a coma, days went by until her children had to make decision to keep her on life support in intensive care or pull the plug.

My grandmother came to me one morning and asked me to pray for my aunt. My grandmother knew who to come to in regard to petitioning Heaven for a response and healing breakthrough. She herself experienced the miraculous power of God through the power of faith and prayer agreement when she asked me to pray, touch, and agree for a miracle. God healed my grandmother twice from cancer and kidney disease through me praying, prophesying over her, and giving her my personal prayer shawl to sleep with for seven days—and doing so she received her own healing both times.

Therefore, when she came to me this time I thought she was in need of another healing miracle; but it wasn't for her, it was for my great aunt, her cousin. They were like sisters even though they were first cousins. She began to tell me about the decision the family had to make and that they were getting together soon probably to cease her life support. This decision to be made bothered me so deeply. This was the very first time I was in a situation to pray for God's breakthrough power. I did what my grandmother asked of me, but I did not pray for just a miracle *per se,* but a sign that God's will be done and that He would display His sovereignty in this situation.

As a recognized and respected emerging prophetic leader and governmental minister in the Body of Christ, I wanted to inquire of the Lord in this matter, not by my own will triggered by my emotions, but solely on God. I wanted clearance from Him personally to see if this was actually His will in the matter. I prayed earnestly for my great aunt, I began to decree the Word of God over her, and I declared for the Lord's will to be done—whether she lives or transitions, but not at the decision of her family or children. I inquired of the Lord to show me a sign personally from Heaven that He had heard my supplication and petition.

PRAYERS ANSWERED BY HEAVEN

Did you know that Heaven has ears? Angels have ears as well. The Bible says angels belongs to Him who carries out God's commands and who are obedient to the sound of His words (see Psalm 103:20). Angels sent by the Lord on your behalf only respond to God's Word to carry out His will in the affairs of His people. You have to give voice to your healing confessions and commands through your vocal cords of faith and from Heaven's perspective. Faith activated me to believe for my great aunt's miracle breakthrough even when she did not have enough faith for herself. I went to the Courts of Heaven on my aunt's behalf and had my family's decision overridden and vetoed. I stood as a prophetic intercessor and went to the Power of Attorney and Judge—Jesus—to make a swift execution judgment, and verdict. Meanwhile, in my prayer time, I began to prophetically release heavenly decrees and commands that God's will be demonstrated. Heaven responds to the prayers of the righteous (see James 5:16).

We are seated in heavenly places with Christ Jesus here and now (see Ephesians 2:6). I was about 21 years of age at the time, making prophetic decrees and declarations as a prophet. But I knew the authority that I walked in by the Word of God as a young believer and prophetic minister. It was always my heart and passion to see God's will displayed in any 911 emergency cases. Moreover, my prayer for my great aunt was not for her to live another 10–20 years, but my prayer was that her life would be orchestrated by God—not taken by man. I know there are financial burdens and responsibilities that come with hospital stays. The invoice can be astronomical if there is no health insurance in place. Personally, I knew I had been given authority in

Christ to command things to turn around, so I activated my faith in prayer by speaking the word of faith to command my aunt's situation to bring glory to the Father.

Furthermore, I inquired of the Lord all night Friday for God to do something unpredicted, unprecedented, and uncalculated. The family was going to pull the plug on Saturday morning around 9 A.M. I prayed and decreed that God's will would be executed and for Him to blow my family's finite minds. I wanted my family to know the God of miracles and who does miracles. My twin brother Naim, mother, and grandmother all knew that I was standing in the gap, praying for a supernatural outcome and sign for Aunt Pauline. Suddenly, at 12 midnight, I received a prayer breakthrough and release in my spirit while weeping before the Lord for her all night.

When Saturday morning came, my mother and grandmother returned home from the hospital. I was sure to hear the worse at first or to hear something negative, but to my surprise there was sudden peace, joy, and happiness on both of their faces. My mother told me that when the family got to the hospital to finally pull the plug and to say their goodbyes, my aunt came out of the coma, sat up in her bed, and began to talk, smile, and eat as if she was never in a comatose state. This was an overnight wonder. This is what I call a miracle breakthrough by the power of prayer agreement and prophetic commands and declarations. I was totally elated and stoked about the news.

God heard my prayers and answered my supplication from Heaven. His sovereignty and supernatural intervention far exceeded my faith expectations. I had to speak to my aunt's mountain and command it by faith to be removed in Jesus' name in prayer. My aunt could not speak to her own mountain by faith, so I did it for her! Sometimes it will take the faith of others for you to receive your healing breakthrough. Just like the four men who took the man sick with the palsy up a staircase and tore off the roof for the man to receive his healing from Jesus. Jesus saw their faith to do the impossible for someone else (see Mark 2:1-9). I talk more about faith later in the following chapters in this book.

HEAVEN'S INTERVENTION

When initially hearing the bad news of my aunt's condition, I wanted to get a second opinion from the Lord. I was not settled in my spirit that on Saturday morning her life should hang in the balance based on man's decision instead of God's primarily. Nevertheless, I realized that her life was ultimately in the hands of the Lord. It was my passion to command a change in the situation in prayer. I heard a saying that prayer changes things, but I will go on to say that *prayer changes everything.*

My personal encounter with God allowed me to know that at the end of the day, God has the final say. I may have been a little selfish in the matter, but my selfishness in wanting to see her defeat the odds caused me to act on it in prayer. I believe that we have to be very selfish when it comes to healing, to the things of God and His will outlined in His Word. I did not give up on my great aunt because I realized that it is not about me, but God concerning her. Consequently, I had to think of myself as if I were in her situation; I would want someone to command in prayer for things to change on my behalf. I wanted my aunt to know that I believed she could live and not die—but in God's timing, not in man's.

Moreover, several months after coming out of the coma, my great aunt finally went home to be with the Lord. I was saddened by the news but I realized that God is in control and she went home at His timing, not man's. I understand what it is like to pray for others and see God work miracle after miracle. It is an amazing feeling to know that someone has your best interest at heart.

Personally, on February 6, 2016, my jaw was broken due to an unexpected assault. The doctor x-rayed the area and stated, "Mr. Collins, your jaw is fractured and it's considered to be broken. You will need emergency surgery as soon as possible." I was saying to the Lord, "God, not right now, I have preaching engagements coming up, this is a tremendous setback for me." The enemy wanted to shut the mouth of God's prophet. I just could not afford to be out of service for that long recovering, and especially did not want to go under the knife.

In addition, I did not want any surgical scars on my face and definitely did not want my jaw wired. The doctor explained my only two options were to get an incision surgery to install metal plates or get my jaw wired. Either option would require 6–12 weeks for total healing. I sensed the Lord telling me to get the incision surgery for the plate. Meanwhile, there were hundreds of people praying for me on Facebook, Twitter, Instagram, and other social media platforms when they heard what happened. I finally decided to go with the surgery to have metal plates and screws installed to adjust and correct my jaw. The surgery was scheduled for the following Monday, and my decision was made that Thursday morning prior to surgery.

PERSONAL MIRACLE FROM GOD

Over the course of the weekend prior to my surgery, I received numerous prophetic words that God was going to do a miracle. I believe the word of prophecy, and being a man of faith, I began to lay hands on the left side of my jaw and began to boldly command in Jesus' name the Word of God, word of faith, and what I believe Heaven wanted to do for me. I took action and came into agreement with Heaven on earth with radical faith. I did not want to sit back and let things happen to me; rather, I wanted to command my jaw to obey the Word of the Lord and be healed in Jesus' name. Nevertheless, Monday morning came; I had my successful surgery, which was three and a half hours long.

Interestingly, a week later after my surgery it was a national holiday, so my follow-up with the doctors was on Tuesday, which was the day the stitches would be removed. While home recovering until my next follow-up, God did exactly what He had spoken through prophetic leaders—that I would receive a miracle in seven days. The following Tuesday morning, the doctors did a follow-up x-ray and lo and behold the fractured jaw was totally healed. The fractured jaw near my ear looked like it never happened. The damaged bone was totally restored as new.

One may ask, "Well, if God did the miracle, why did you undergo surgery in the first place?" The answer to that question is that when my jaw was still damaged, the plate was installed to correct the jaw alignment and to stabilize my jaw. There was another part of my jaw that was cracked where no plate was placed because of the location. That part of the bone had to heal on its own, usually taking months to heal totally. Just as a leg or arm bone takes a very long time to fully heal. Well in my case, that bone in seven days was not only healed but it looked like there was never a crack in it from the impact. The before and after x-ray images show that there was nothing there. It was a work of God.

The power of the spoken word, the prayer of faith, and action on my part to lay hands on myself, to command healing to take place while standing on the report of Dr. Jesus brought healing. Just seven days after the surgery I was able to chew, speak, eat, and even do things that would not have been normally possible to do. God strengthened me instantly and what normally takes 6–8 weeks to recover, God did in seven days. We know that the number seven is the number of completion, perfection, and God's divine number. What am I saying? Heaven is declaring your total complete healing today.

In Part Two of this book you will find a 90-day healing devotional and prayer confessions and commands to prophetically speak aloud to inspire you to release your faith for receiving instantaneous healing during rough times that you may be facing and enduring to see changing results by the power of the spoken words. Something we do or say may look foolish to the unspiritual or carnal, but when you are in need of a miracle or healing, you will do whatever it takes—especially if someone tells you how to receive it. Faith commands of healing will create an atmosphere for healing by what you speak (command).

FAITH HAS EARS

The Bible says in Romans 10:17 (NASB), *"Faith comes from hearing, and hearing by the word of Christ."* What are you hearing in your ears? Are they faith-provoking words of life and change? What is Heaven commanding you to decree and release? It has been said that God allows people to go through sickness, illnesses, and traumatic things to teach them a lesson. I come to let you know that is far from the truth. God does not have to break my jaw to get my attention or cause sickness and disease to occur to cause me to change, repent, or give in. Let me be emphatically clear: Sickness, disease, demons, and the like are *not* the will of God and *not* the culture of Heaven. God does *not* afflict people with sickness nor does He need to teach us any life lessons to obey Him through the means of sickness or disease.

There may be things that people may be born with or have inherited that God will use for His glory to bring about healing. However, it is never God's agenda or motive to inflict anyone with sickness or disease. God's will is to see you healed, delivered, and made whole. He has given His church spiritual gifts for that purpose to be the extension of Heaven on earth to bring about long-lasting results. That is the purpose and agenda of Heaven, why Jesus was sent to the earth. He came to destroy the works of satan (see 1 John 3:8). God has a work and satan has a work as well. God's work is the supernatural power of healing, and satan's work is sickness, sin, disease, and spirit of infirmities. People perish not because of demons, sickness, disease, or incurable illness—they perish due to lack of knowledge.

COMMAND SICKNESS TO OBEY YOU

When I first started in public ministry at the age of 17, I had a mighty prayer warrior and intercessory prophet who was my first administrator, who was later diagnosed with breast cancer. She was a woman of tremendous faith, but her faith was rocked due to the cancer diagnosis and she felt her life was being cut short. If you knew her or saw her in person, you would never think that she was suffering because of her strong appearance and she didn't look ill. Arlene would oftentimes ask me and my twin brother, Naim, to come over to her home to pray for her because she felt hopeless. So we would pray earnestly and fervently, but nothing would happen. She would call about every other week to give us an update, which would stir up something inside me and my brother; we knew we needed to visit her. This was the Holy Spirit boldness and discontentment needed to see cancer defeated.

We would go to Arlene's home and lay hands on her and command the cancer in her to leave her body in Jesus' name. Furthermore, we had to command by speaking directly to the cancer and to the white blood cells to reproduce and multiple rapidly to fight off the disease—declaring that her body is the temple of the Holy Spirit. We had to speak to the spirit of infirmities, trauma, unforgiveness, death, and vital organs to hear the Word of the Lord. We knew that there was spiritual warfare over her destiny, and her life was on the line. She needed us like never before. We needed to remind cancer and the spirit of death whose body (house) it belonged to.

One day we took authority over what was plaguing Arlene's body and we spoke to cancer directly and served cancer its final eviction notice, in Jesus' name. Several weeks later, we received a phone call from Arlene. We initially thought she was going to tell us a bad report or follow-up. However, she called rejoicing and elated that the Lord did a miracle for her. The doctors could not find any trace of cancer in her body and blood!

When you command and order something to happen, you expect that response immediately. Commands are given to those who have been authorized to give orders, commands, and directives. Sometimes things in our lives just need a little order to it to bring healing breakthrough, peace, and joy.

This was a great praise report that as Spirit-filled believers we can command sickness, diseases, and anything tormenting us to go. She was strong enough to believe the Word of God that she pulled on others to touch and agree with her. She birthed a prayer movement ministry called "Touch and Agree Ministries." Unfortunately, 12 years later Arlene Brown, after being a cancer survivor, went home to be with the Lord after battling cancer for the second time, which came back aggressively.

Sometimes things will come back with vengeance, but we must be as aggressive as well and fight back harder. I was there until the end with her, and I saw how strong she was, knowing that because God healed her the first time, He could surely do it again. It hurt me to be there in hospice on her final days as she transitioned to the Father. She believed God for her healing even until the end; and I dedicated this book to her and those who believe God for healing and miracles. At the time of writing this book, she gave me permission to tell her story and wanted you, the reader, to know that you can command you are healed here and now!

CHAPTER 3

Strong and Healthy Christian Believers

Nevertheless, I will bring health and healing to it; I will heal my people and will let them enjoy abundant peace and security (Jeremiah 33:6 NIV).

God wants to heal His people so He can raise up strong and healthy Christian believers. It is one thing to be healthy, but it is another to be strong. I can be healthy but not strong. God wants His people to be strong and healthy so we can grow in leap and bounds in Christ through the Holy Spirit. God desires to take us on a healing journey to recovery and wholeness that will release the faith we need to demand the spiritual results we are anticipating. The Father wants to change our natural and spiritual condition by the very words we speak. If we believe and speak that we are sick and tired, then over time we will become sick and tired. Our words carry creative abilities.

Our decisions create and shape our destinies. There is a saying I used to hear when I was young: "We are what we eat," which is true. And I would go a little further and say, *"We are what we speak and think."* We must condition our minds to believe we are healed and speak out what we believe in our hearts. We must recondition our minds on God's healing truth in His Word and prophetically declare it so, in Jesus' name. We must feast on the truth through God's living Word that will sustain us, heal us, and deliver us. I always say, *"Faith is your healing prescription that will cause you to bounce back and overcome life's obstacles—spiritually, mentally, and physically."* Jesus declares that the words that He speaks are Spirit-life. What are we speaking out of our mouths? What do we believe? What are we hearing that is influencing us? I was always told by men of faith to believe the Word of God, no matter what. Hold God to His promises.

GOD'S MEDICINE FOR HEALING

God's promises over our lives are yes and amen. God's medicine for you is found in His Word. You have to *confess* the Word of God over your life daily, which is as essential as eating, drinking, and sleeping (rest). It is God's will for you to be healthy! I do not care what the doctors have declared. God has the last and final word! Heaven is declaring your healing and miracle today. What is a healing? In Webster's New World Dictionary, the word "heal" means "to make or become well or healthy again, to cure (a disease) or mend as a wound." In addition, the word "health" means "physical and mental well-being, freedom from disease, condition of body or mind, wish for one's health and happiness." It is the heartbeat and DNA of Heaven to see you completely free and in good health—not only mentally, but also physically, and most of all spiritually.

The Bible is clear in regard to healing and erasing every erroneous notion of deception that God will punish His people with sickness to teach them a valuable lesson. Alternatively, I have heard that to have tremendous anointing on one's life, overcoming sickness or disease is a prerequisite to a powerful ministry. That is not true. Neither Jesus nor any of His disciples and apostles needed to be healed first from sickness to heal others. I believe people who have been sick or ill and then God heals them miraculously has a supernatural advantage and faith to receive faith for others to overcome their conditions. Sickness and disease is not the culture of Heaven and God's judgment on humanity.

The Bible reveals that healing and health is His will for believers. God is a healer and He has already made clear provision for our healing through His Word. Psalm 107:20 declares that *His Word will bring healing*, and that *God's Word will never fail, pass away and lose it power* according to Proverbs 4:20-22.

HEALING PRESCRIPTION BY DAILY CONFESSIONS AND COMMANDS

In addition, Jesus Himself taught His disciples that the Kingdom of God works like a person who plants seeds, which is the Word of God, and His Word contains supernatural ingredients and quality (read Luke 8:11). What does His Word contain? It contains life and resurrection power! Later in this book, in Part Two, there is a powerful prayer starter, Scripture references, a personal prophetic Word from Daddy God, and a daily antidote to start your day empowered, equipped, inspired, relieved, healed, delivered, and blessed.

As you read and declare the faith confessions and commands of healing each day, it will be like a seed, which may appear not to be alive or working—but it is. The seed of health comes to relieve you of your pain, and over time you will become stronger, healthier, and even cured of the condition you face. God will heal you from every emotional, physical, mental, and spiritual symptom that persists in your life. God wants to see you whole in mind, body, and soul.

In the next 90 days, allow the Holy Spirit to minister to you; read the faith confessions and commands of healing aloud with authority and with strength through the Holy Spirit. These prophetic declarations of healing on the pages are full of God's supernatural power. They are the Father's divine medicine through His Word for you to take daily. Take them by reading, commanding, and confessing these words regularly without becoming impatient. You must understand that things may get worse before they get better, as you become aware of your shortcomings and yearn more to obey God's will for a better life for you.

Over the next 90 days, I believe God will do spiritual "soul surgery" and "soul therapy" that will bring about healing and the miracle that you have been asking for from the Father. Whose report are you going to believe? Jesus still works miracles and healing today. It is not a thing of the past, it's a thing of today!

If the pain persists, then double the dosage of God's Word and release it until you see results. I want to be very clear in regard to those who are waiting on God for healing and are still taking their medication prescribed by their doctor. If you are taking medication, never stop taking your medication without seeking the direction and consultation of your personal doctor. God gives us wisdom; and even though we are believing God for a miracle and healing, we must use wisdom while the healing is taking place. It is not wisdom to stop taking any medication until it is confirmed you are healed by a doctor or medical specialist.

FAITH THAT PRODUCES EVIDENCE

The Bible says, *"Now faith is the substance of things hope for, the evidence of things not seen"* (Hebrews 11:1). Release your faith to see the evidence taking root in you. I love what the Bible also says, that we are to confess our sins one to another and be healed (see James 5:16). There may be things that have become subtle blockages for our divine breakthroughs and healing. When I was young and I knew I did something wrong, when I eventually confessed my wrongdoing, I always felt better. It was as if the world was lifted off my shoulders. I did not have to carry the guilt or shame or secret. Confessing to someone else allowed me to free myself and be held accountable.

There is nothing to gain by holding things in that are eating at us spiritually. Confessing personal sins and acts of disobedience to the Lord frees us from any guilt, pain, injury, curse, and sickness. We are to host and become conduits of healing power and glory, not sickness, disease, and unrepented acts of sins. There are things that keep us sick and bound.

Oftentimes it's not sickness or demons, it's our very own decisions that keep us bound and can become open doors for curses, sickness, and disease to exist in our lives. Trusted accountability and submitted to a local, sound, Bible-teaching church will help us on our way to joy, peace, and righteousness in the Holy Spirit. Transparency, forgiveness, and honesty are keys to healing and deliverance.

God does not make us do anything; He has given us free will. Our destinies are determined by our decisions that should be guided and directed by the Holy Spirit daily. Governing our thoughts and actions through truth and Holy-Spirit empowerment can cause us to walk in total healing. Where we are today, I believe, resulted from what we decided to do with our lives.

Nothing just happens to us; we decide to allow or permit things to happen. I do believe, though, there are some circumstances that are out of our control.

REVERSING THE CONDITION

If a doctor tells me that too much sugar is not good for me and I need to cut back, I have two choices. One, I can choose to continue to consume sugar; or two, I can take the doctor's advice and cut back. There are many things we must admit are not good for us and change bad habit into good ones for the better. It's never too late. We can reverse our condition with the truth of God's Word and get the best results possible. We can weigh our options with God's healing facts through His Word. We decide our healing path by faith. God want us to make godly decisions through godly wisdom. We are what we eat, think, and believe!

What are we saying in our hearts that is allowing us to become that very thing? Let us make sure we do *not* become couriers of sickness, unforgiveness, bitterness, resentment, shame, guilt, victimization, depression, oppression, and sin. Let us instead make sure we become couriers of the healing power of God.

There may be many or various things that I may have not mentioned that are causing us to encounter unfortunate conditions. I know that the enemy will fight those whom God has called to do great exploits for Him, because they poise a lethal threat to the kingdom of darkness. That is why intercession, fasting, and prayer are keys to releasing the angelic armies of Heaven to contend on our behalf. Even how people mistreat their parents, guardians, and even those in authority can be open doors and legal ground for sickness, curses, and disease to exist that needs to be addressed through forgiveness, repentance, renouncing, and reconciliation.

I heard a story by a ministry friend of mine that a man of God from Chicago, who had a powerful healing ministry, would see healing results instantly. And people could not understand his method of healing. He had "reckless faith," in that he would use strong words and even threats to cause a person to receive a miracle or healing from God. For example, he told a person that if he did not get up from the wheelchair and walk, that he would

31

go over and kick the person's you-know-what. I believe the threat caused the person to believe for the miracle and choose to be healed instead of being forced to walk.

Now this approach may not be the friendliest or even seem Christlike, but who are we to judge the method and strange ways of getting supernatural results. The point and glory to the name of God is that through this man's reckless faith healing method, everyone was supernaturally healed and received their breakthrough. I guess they took the man seriously and did not want to suffer any consequences for not listening to his instructions or commands.

The point I am making with this example is that the healing evangelist was bold and tapped into a vein of discontentment of seeing people bound, sick, and diseased. His discontentment created disdain against sickness, disease, illness, and spirits of infirmities. What has caused you to be disgusted and discontented about which causes you to respond in unusual faith, radical faith, or, like the evangelist in reckless faith, to see the better outcome for yourself and others? You can do the same as well for yourself.

THE SPIRIT OF IGNORANCE

Moreover, bad eating habits and patterns can cause sickness and diseases in our physical bodies. Ignorance of generational bloodline curses can be opened through acts of iniquity of a particular bloodline sin. Generational curses are passed down from generation to generation. When we are saved, we are no longer held responsible for ancestral sins passed down. They are broken at the finished work of the cross through Jesus and at conversion, but they can be accessed through legal rights given to us through sin. I do not address generational curses and curses in this book, I suggest that you read my book, *Prophetic Breakthrough: Decrees that Break Curses and Release Blessings* to learn more about generational curses.

We must arm ourselves with biblical truth, prophetic revelation by the Spirit, and knowledge to disarm error, ignorance, and deception. Remember that it is ignorance that causes people to perish. The enemy knows that if he can keep God's people walking in ignorance, then he can short-circuit their life-expectancy and fulfilling their God-given purpose and destiny.

God wants to heal many of us, but we must be willing to give up some things that may be killing us. We may be doing things out of ignorance that bring us harm. This book will become a spiritual nurse and pain management remedy to help you on your path to total spiritual enrichment, nourishment, empowerment, recovery, and healing. It will serve as a spiritual rehab that will bring you to a place of personal revival.

DAILY BENEFITS OF HEALING

The following are a few benefits of declaring, commanding, and confessing healing over you through God's Word:

God will help you:

So we say with confidence, "The Lord is my helper; I will not be afraid. What can mere mortals do to me?" (Hebrews 13:6 NIV)

God will strengthen the weak:

Beat your plowshares into swords and your pruning hooks into spears. Let the weakling say, "I am strong!" (Joel 3:10 NIV)

God will keep His promise concerning you:

Yet he did not waver through unbelief regarding the promise of God, but was strengthened in his faith and gave glory to God, being fully persuaded that God had power to do what he had promised (Romans 4:20-21 NIV).

God will redeem you from the curse of the law:

Christ redeemed us from the curse of the law by becoming a curse for us, for it is written: "Cursed is everyone who is hung on a pole" (Galatians 3:13 NIV).

God's Word heals:

He sent out his word and heal them; he rescued them from the grave (Psalm 107:20 NIV).

God through His Son, Jesus borne our sickness:

Surely he took up our pain and bore our suffering, yet we considered him punished by God, stricken by him, and afflicted. But he was pierced for our transgressions, he was crushed for our iniquities; the punishment that brought us peace was on him, and by his wounds we are healed (Isaiah 53:4-5 NIV).

God will cause the spirit of death to pass over you:

Get rid of the old yeast, so that you may be a new unleavened batch—as you really are. For Christ, our Passover lamb, has been sacrificed (1 Corinthians 5:7 NIV).

We must be confident in the Word of God and the Great Physician—Jesus Christ. We must understand that Jesus has paid an ultimate price for our healing. He purchased it with His own blood and sacrificed His life for you and I on the cross as a reparation or expiation for our sin. We must not allow our healing to be taken away from us. Speak the confessions of healing out your mouth while you read and allow the seed to be sown and cultivated in your heart and plant it in your spiritual walk.

These are not mere words that I just made up. These are powerful tools for the Christian believer to quote, and read the affirmation of Scriptures in Part Two: 90-Day Devotional and Activation Confessions and Commands that Unleash Healing. The faith confessions should be spoken aloud in Jesus' name. You must command your body, mind, soul, finances, emotions, and even demon spirits of infirmities to do what you say by the authority of the Word of God, in Jesus' name and as child of the King.

You must know, without any doubt, of the heartbeat of Jesus when it comes to receiving your total healing. God wants to see you fully healed and anew.

Even though Jesus paid it all physically for us to be healed physically, there are still sick and diseased Christian believers. I believe that there are simple steps that people can take to receive their healing breakthrough. As believers, we have to be faith-possessors when it comes to healing—*believers* in the healing power of God. And we must be persuaded in our hearts that God in fact wants us healed and it's His will for us. If a person does not believe that, then 9 of 10 will not be healed.

Jesus had declared countless times throughout the gospel to those in need of a miracle, healing, and breakthrough to just believe or have faith. The fear of the supernatural and doubt of the healing ministry of Jesus has to be broken off the mind-sets of those who profess Christ as Lord. Jesus still is in the healing and miracle business. Throughout His earthly ministry, we see Him healing, working miracles, raising the dead, teaching the gospel, and casting out evil spirits.

Psalm 103:2-3 says, *"Bless the Lord, O my soul, and forget not all His benefits: who forgives all your iniquities, who heals all your diseases."* I love this passage of Scripture. Why? The writer is acknowledging the Lord who forgives sins and who heals *all* diseases. It does not say that God will forgive some sins and heal some diseases—it emphatically says *all* iniquities are forgiven and *all* diseases are healed. What a great benefit to know that God will heal all your diseases and forgive all of your sins. That is a benefit I do not think anyone wants to forget.

As Christian believers, to receive total victory over what we are facing in our body, mind, and soul, we must also believe in the covenant promises of the Lord when it comes to healing His people. God loves and wants to heal; and in fact, He is looking for those who are in dire need of a healing and a miracle breakthrough.

HEALING MEDITATION IS SPIRITUAL MEDICATION

We must declare what the Father wants to do in our lives by professing it boldly, confessing them outwardly, declaring, and establishing them prophetically. You must know for sure that God will and wants to heal not only you, but also everyone. It is like when you first gave your life and heart to

Christ, you believed that He lived, died, was buried, and on the third day was resurrected with all power over sin, death, and the grave for you. This was something you confessed with your whole heart, mind, and soul with your mouth that caused you to become a born-again believer of Christ.

Likewise, with healing and receiving your miracle, you must believe in your heart that all your sins are forgiven and all your sickness or disease is healed, because that is why Jesus died for you, so that you may live and have eternal life after this life.

Furthermore, as you read this book and apply the prayers, healing confessions, and prophetic messages from the Father, begin to meditate on what you have read. The Hebrew form or expression of *meditation* or *meditating* is "to mumble the words out loud." In other words, mumble forth or speak forth through meditating the promises of God over your life for healing. You must know and take personally the promises of God. I always say, *"Meditation on God's Word is your spiritual medication."*

Permit the Holy Spirit to allow you to meditate (mumble) each day for the next 90 days what is the promises of the Lord for your life. As you read each healing confession and command set forth, personalize them for you to mumble aloud and seize the moment of healing that belongs to you. Do not believe the lies of the enemy that healing and miracles are not for today. That is far from the truth. Healing is *your* inheritance. You not only are going to meditate (mumble) by speaking what you will walk in, but command it boldly!

Healing is a part of the Kingdom and nature of God. Muzzle out the lie and confess the truth of your healing with your mouth. Establish it each day with healing confessions that will bring out the best result possible. You must have faith that healing has happened, before we ever see it. The Bible says, *"Now faith is the substance of the things hope for and the evidence of things not seen"* (Hebrews 11:1). What are you hoping for? It requires "now faith" to activate the evidence of the things you are hoping for and expecting to come into being for you.

Healing takes a process to come into divine manifestation. We tend to get healing and miracles mixed up or think they are the same. Healing and miracles are different. Healing is a progressive miracle; a miracle is an instant healing. I believe that *faith is the substance of things hope for—and without faith, fear becomes a substance abuser.*

For example, if a person was in an accident and is treated and then in recovery, medications are prescribed to take daily in order to receive full healing. Over time, the person will return to normal. But if a person was in a terrible accident and became paralyzed, then the condition is critical and the person is in need of a miracle. It doesn't matter what medications are provided for pain management, when the person recovers from the initial injury, he or she may be healed in some parts of the body, but still unable to walk. This person not only needs to be wholly healed, but also needs the strength of the Lord to continue their Christian walk and live a full life again.

Just because a person declares that they are healed many times doesn't mean that a healing and miracle will instantly happen. There are individuals I know who will confess they are healed but physically they are not, and most of the time they really do not believe what they are declaring or speaking in their heart. As faith believers, we must get into a faith realm in God to believe in our heart what God's promises are, and then we can declare boldly with our mouths. Confessing with our mouths what is in our minds and speaking from our hearts is key to our healing breakthrough.

THINK HEALING AND YOU WILL BE HEALED

The Bible says, *"For as he thinks in his heart, so is he"* (Proverbs 23:7). In other words, you are what you think. The Father wants His people to become more "healed conscious" than "sick conscious." I believe we must have an "already healed" mentality to set in motion the manifestation of healing so that we speak it forth in faith. The Bible also says, *"out of the abundance of the heart the mouth speaks"* (see Matthew 12:34; Luke 6:45). We have to meditate, confess, read, and study the Word of God that pertains to healing and the ministry of healing through Jesus, and ask the Holy Spirit to teach us the principle of healing and the Kingdom.

Oftentimes, people give up on their own personal healing because they do not see instant results. Yet who goes to the gym to get into better shape and expects a total transformation overnight? On the other hand, what farmer plants seeds in cultivated soil and expects a great harvest overnight? It is a gradual process to obtain the result that you made up in your mind to receive. See results by commanding, ordering, and speaking to that mountain daily until it becomes a valley.

Likewise, with healing and the word of healing in God's Word. There are times when people are instantly healed, which are called miracles; and a processed miracle is a healing. However, we must understand that if we are healed instantly or gradually healed, what will we do if the symptom comes back or reoccurs? Will you give up by accepting the sickness or disease? Or will you fight back and do the necessary actions to destroy the works of satan?

It's the design of the enemy to rob you of your joy, peace, sanity, and righteous living. He wants to steal, kill, and destroy. But Jesus, on the other hand, comes to bring eternal life and abundant living (see John 10:10). You must know that the enemy will always attack when you are at your most vulnerable place. Some in healing and deliverance ministries have a habit and make the mistake at times of diagnosing the symptoms instead of activating the prognosis by casting out the evil spirits. We have to do both: identify the problem and evict the problem as well. Jesus came not only to *diagnose* us but also give us the healing solution, which is the *prognosis*.

JESUS LOVES TO SEE YOU HEALED AND MADE WHOLE

When I pray someone's miracle, healing, and breakthrough, I must be honest and know that I cannot do anything without Holy Spirit guidance and that I am not the healer. I also know that it's not in my name that a person I am praying for is healed, but in the name of Jesus only! It is Jesus Himself, through me by the Holy Spirit, who is working the miracle or healing. Whenever it's me and not Christ, then there is no results.

The primary source and ingredient to healing is love and compassion. Jesus, seeing a large crowd, had compassion on them and healed their sick according to Matthew 14:14. Furthermore, there was a blind man in the

Word of God who confessed that Jesus was "Lord" without ever seeing Him personally working a miracle or healing. The blind men received healing by faith, by hearing about the healing that Jesus performed. In other words, they "heard" what He had done to others, and when they heard Jesus was passing by, they cried out saying His name to get His attention.

I am reminded in the natural when someone stays too long and we want them to leave. We go to court to have the person removed from our residence. The court issues and serves a 90-day notice of eviction, legally by a constable.

Likewise, I prophetically speak that the eviction notice is issued and served to *all* sickness, disease, oppression, spirit of infirmities, death, and depression that is causing reoccurring pain or suffering to vacant your spiritual premises. Today, Jesus is healing and setting you free. During the next 90 days, embrace the river of love that is flowing to you and through you by the Holy Spirit.

My question for you today: After finishing this book, will you be the ambassador and commander of healing who will declare the healing promises of God? If you answered yes, then you are on your way. Do not give up when you don't see instant results, persevere until you see and feel better. I challenge you to try the Father at His Word. Remind God of His promises regarding healing and recite them out loud to assure Him you are in agreement with each one. I break off of you every shame, guilt, and any regret due to any sickness or condition you may be experiencing.

JUST SPEAK THE WORD

God did not curse you or cause you to go through this to teach you something or He is mad at you by allowing such things to happen. We must understand that things in life happen that are out of our control and something may have been a consequence of things that we may be ignorant of. Today is the day to *arise* out of life's rut and soar above the odds. You are a winner, and today is your day for your miracle and healing.

There is an account in the Word of God about a Roman Centurion who had an ill servant. The centurion went to Jesus needing His assistance to heal the servant boy. Jesus offered to go to the centurion's house to perform a healing, but the Roman soldier suggested that Jesus could perform the healing at a distance instead. The man said to Jesus, *"Lord, I am not worthy that You should come under my roof. But only speak a word, and my servant will be healed"* (Matthew 8:8).

We can see that the centurion obviously believed in Jesus' power and understood the authority that Jesus possessed. If he did not, he would not have come that far to seek Jesus out and to ask Him to perform a healing. This person recognized and understood Jesus for who He is as the One who can just speak and it is done. The Roman centurion had authority, came to Jesus in humility, and subjected himself under Jesus' authority. The second remarkable thing about this man is his faith in the word of Christ and the authority in the word itself that can produce the healing he requested. The point is that this man's faith amazed Jesus because he believed Christ's *words* before he ever saw the *works*.

In other words, He had faith to believe for someone's healing just by the spoken Word of Christ before the healing work ever took place. God wants you to become like the Roman soldier, to believe the commands of healing through the Word of God, to believe for your own healing and miracle before you ever see it manifest. Seeing through the lens of faith gives you access to see your healing and miracle breakthrough before you seize it. The man understood that all Jesus had to do is just *speak* the word, or just *say* the word and it was approved, done, and authorized. Why? Because the man was in authority and had people under his command who obeyed his words. In like manner, the man recognized Jesus was in authority and could command healing to take place for his ill servant, that sickness would respond and obey Jesus regardless of distance.

In prophetic ministry, I have witnessed countless miracles by the mere fact of me prophesying it. There is power in the Word of God. When prophetic words are spoken and sent by faith, angels pick up those prophetic words and carry them out when we give voice to them.

HEALING WINGS

But for you who fear my name, the Sun of Righteousness will rise with healing in his wings. And you will go free, leaping with joy like calves let out to pasture (Malachi 4:2 NLT).

The Sun of Righteousness brings healing in His wings. Your healing will be hand-delivered by Heaven's host of angels. Fresh healing fire is coming to those in need of a supernatural touch by God. As you believe and revere the name of the Lord, He will come like the sun with His healing touch, and you will arise possessing your healing in His wings and be free leaping with joy like calves excited when they are let out of the pasture. I am reminded when I was in elementary school and we could not wait until recess time when the teachers let us out. We were yelling, screaming, running, and so excited to finally get some fresh air and able to play. You will be like little children excited to be finally free by the healing power of God that broke the power of sickness, disease, and pain.

NOW FAITH, NOW HEALED

Jesus was astounded by the centurion's faith that he did not need to see the sign of healing first to believe. The man's faith to travel a distance to Jesus was enough faith in itself, and to ask Jesus to just speak the word. In like manner, we have to just speak, confess, and command healing to take place in our lives in Jesus' name. The centurion found where the Word of God was and faith activated Jesus to perform a miracle.

The first thing most people do when they don't feel well is to find out what's wrong through their family doctor who usually prescribes medication to relieve the pain. In like manner, we can go to the Word of God to give us the antidote to cope with the pain. The centurion went to the Physician named Doctor Jesus to have Him prescribe for the ill servant a dose of healing power that instantly cured his servant.

Most Christian believers today, like the religious leaders of Jesus' day, would rather see a sign first to believe. However, true faith is having and knowing that the evidence of healing is already done without seeing it. Faith has to do with things that are not seen first and the hope of things that are not at hand or evident (see Hebrews 11:1). I believe Jesus commended this man's act of faith in believing in the authority and commands of Jesus' words that activated the healing process. By the time the centurion leader returned home, the boy was totally healed. I believe that *"now faith activates now healings."*

As you *command,* you are healed daily; trust and believe the mere words of healing that the Holy Spirit speaks through you to bring about what you desire. When you command your healing each day, then you can see yourself as the Roman centurion needing Jesus to just speak the word and you know you are healed. Furthermore, picture yourself in the authority of Jesus speaking, commanding, and declaring healing over yourself or for someone else.

READ, RECALL, AND REPEAT— PROPHESY YOUR HEALING DAILY

As you continue to read, remember and repeat aloud the positive healing words daily, and regularly you will allow the truth of God's Word to sink deeply into your heart, which will ultimately change your outcome for the better.

I could not start and finish this book without relating with you and sharing my need of a divine healing from the Lord. I worked the word of faith by commanding myself to be healed, regardless how impossible the situation seemingly appeared. I have come to realize that our situation has to listen to us and obey. There is nothing like Heaven's personal intervention. You are an overcomer and a champion. God is releasing healing angels by your side to bring you the angel food of nourishment to cause you to arise and take up your bed. You are chosen to be a witness and to be a sign and a wonder.

Your very life will be a living testament and epistle of what your God can do. I wrote this book with a sincere passion and heart that *you will* feel better within the first several weeks after speaking life, encouraging yourself in the Lord, and commanding your healing to be so here and now. Even King David at times had to look himself in the mirror of life and encourage himself in the Lord.

Command Your Healing will be the encouraging guide, antidote, and daily prescription of healing by the Holy Spirit, and voice of hope in the chaos of life. Be still and hear the small yet strong voice of the Father declaring His will, intent, and divine purpose over your life. You shall live and not die so as to declare the works of Christ. Today is the start of the greatest days of your life, and I come to touch and agree with you for your total healing, deliverance, and breakthrough. After all, you will become the healing that Heaven has declared over you.

One of my favorite Scriptures on confession is in James 5:16 (NIV), which declares, *"Therefore confess yours sins to each other and pray for each other so that you may be healed. The prayer of a righteous person is powerful and effective."* Can you imagine how many people will receive their healing and miracle if they would simply confess their sins or faults with one to another? As we release our faith with God, pray, and declare openly what we are in need of, Heaven will release it suddenly. The Scripture does not say you might be healed, or it is a possibility that you will be healed, it emphatically states that if we confess our sins and pray for each other that we will or may be healed.

Allow the Holy Spirit to serve you as the compass and roadmap to healing. We are authorized as believers to command things to happen in the power of the name of Jesus. This is not "naming and claiming" but "commanding and confessing" the Word of God. Healing is your inheritance, just as deliverance is the children's bread. It's yours for the taking and your spiritual right as a child of the King.

Are you ready to receive your daily dose of what Heaven has declared today for you? If so, I am elated and am touching and agreeing with you now and for the next 90 days that you will be spiritually and physically transformed and healed from every pain, hurt, disease, illness, sickness, setback, oppression, depressive spirits of guilt, shame, condemnation, and death.

I am here with you, my friend, to see you take up your bed and walk in total victory of what you have "commanded" over your life to see your *healing breakthrough!* After reading through, you may want to share this book with a family member or friend who may need a healing touch from God as well.

CHAPTER 4

Prophesying the Word of Healing

That evening many demon-possessed people were brought to Jesus. He cast out the evil spirits with a simple command, and he healed all the sick. This fulfilled the word of the Lord through the prophet Isaiah, who said, "He took our sicknesses and removed our diseases (Matthew 8:16-17 NLT).

Before I can get into the topic of speaking the word of healing, commanding healing, or confessing our sins, faults, or concerns that bring personal healing, we must first understand simply—what is divine healing? Through this book you will come to understand how to command by possessing your healing—but before we learn and activate that, we must be clear about what divine healing entails.

I believe that a divine healing involves a supernatural intervention or activity that resolves a physical, emotional, or spiritual problem. Moreover, in the Christian paradigm and context, the supernatural element is God who brings about the supernatural intervention and troubleshoots any issue, problem, and condition through the agency of the Holy Spirit.

When I think about divine healing from a Christian, religious perspective, I usually look through the lenses of Jesus' healing ministry by the Gospel narratives. In the New Testament, we can see that one fifth of the Gospels of Matthew, Mark, and Luke is devoted to Jesus' supernatural ministry of healing. At the beginning of Jesus' ministry, the Bible says in Matthew 4:23 that He went throughout Galilee, teaching in their synagogues, preaching the good news of the Kingdom, and healing every disease and sickness among the people. Divine healing was Jesus' primary goal, mission, and agenda for those He met.

What does it mean to prophesy the word of healing? We must first understand the prophetic nature of the Word of God. The Word of God is the final authority and it is infallible. The Old and New Testament Scriptures are prophetic and were penned by prophets and apostles inspired by God.

Second Peter 1:19 (NLT) declares, *"...we have even greater confidence in the message proclaimed by the prophets. You must pay close attention to what they wrote, for their words are like a lamp shining in a dark place—until the Day dawns, and Christ the Morning Star shines in your hearts."*

The Word of God is a sure word of prophecy and like a lamp shining in dark places. In our prophetic activation sessions in prophetic training, we teach the students to prophesy the Word of God to those to whom they are ministering. They are waiting and listening for God to give them a word of knowledge concerning a condition or physical impression on the body that needs to be healed and then they will find a Bible verse or Scripture passage and release a prophetic word—and the healing anointing is released through prophecy.

In the school that I founded and oversee, The Prophetic Academy, we not only activate students in hearing the voice of God but also in speaking as the oracles of God to release the healing as well. The Bible shares an important element about the prophetic: that without prophetic revelation, divine guidance, vision, and prophecy, the people cast off order, are scattered, and are made naked and ashamed (see Proverbs 29:18). There is power in prophecy! I have witnessed tremendous healing breakthroughs through a prophetic word. Prophesying the written word of God of healing by faith will produce the results that the receiver is looking for. Faith comes by hearing and hearing the prophetic message by the prophets in God's Word.

We have the ability to prophesy by decreeing healing over ourselves and those who are in need of a healing intervention. Prophesying is simply speaking by inspiration the Word of God by faith. I did not want to get into healing by the Word of God without covering briefly the term "prophesying" and what it means. In the Hebrew Old Testament, the customary words for prophet and prophesying are *nabi* and *naba*, apparently from a root meaning "to flow forth."

Many Hebrew prophets and the apostolic New Testament writers and scribes were preeminently expositors of the divine will of God. They were great communicators of God's will, counsel, intent and purpose to humanity. Prophesying is not limited to just the prophets *per se* but that the function of prophesying was entirely an accepted means of speaking for God, interpreting His will to others, and publicly expounding or preaching by prophetic revelation God's mind, will, and agenda. Prophesying was not tacitly limited to New Testament prophesying, to mere preaching. There is a difference in prophesying by a prophet and prophetic preaching and teaching. In other words, there is a difference between inspired knowledge due to application and prophetic revelation given by God to His prophets and apostles (see Galatians 1:14-16; Ephesians 3:3-5).

There is an inspired utterance through the Holy Spirit to speak the will of God. God's will is His written Word; and through the prophetic, we can articulate divine revelation by speaking plainly God's intention to those in need of a healing or breakthrough. We are declaring prophetically healing by faith for God's will to be done in a person's life. I have personally experienced healing through prophecy and transformation through the prophetic Word of God. It was my faith to believe the prophecy that caused Heaven to respond on my behalf. I am a prophecy fulfilled that was in motion as spoken through the mouth of God's prophets and anointed prophetic ministers. The prophetic gift and ministry is needed in today's society to bring transformation.

We know that prophecy is for the believer. Can you imagine the benefit it can bring to those who need to know Jesus Christ as their personal Savior? Prophesying is to simply speak and declare the heart, mind, and will of God to His people. I have seen supernatural things happen when the gift of the Holy Spirit is activated and the believer's faith is stretched to be a vessel of the supernatural. God wants to speak and prophesy through you, whether you are called to the ministry office of a prophet or not. Every

Spirit-filled believer can prophesy! So why not activate in the realm of prophesying healing.

JESUS THE SIN DESTROYER

First John 3:8 (NIV) says, *"The one who does what is sinful is of the devil, because the devil has been sinning from beginning. The reason the Son of God appeared was to destroy the devil's work."*

As we can see from the Scripture in First John 3, the sinful nature is the nature of the devil who has been sinning from the beginning of time. And it was the Father's commission to send His only begotten Son to destroy the works of satan by demonstrating the supernatural and deliverance works of the Father. Due to sin, Adam (and all humankind) forfeited their privilege to live forever. Humankind was created to live forever, but through disobedience they (Adam and Eve) were evicted from the Garden of Eden (see Genesis 3:21-24). They are now subject to the natural elements, which they were not previously subject to. God's original plan and design for humans included eternal life of a covenant fellowship with the Father—divine wholeness and healing, spiritual, and physical prosperity. When God created humanity, He provided to them His attributes and authority, which is to be displayed and executed in the earth realm.

Sin is what creates a separation between humankind and God and His original plan and purpose for their lives. Jesus Christ came to destroy the works of satan and to restore humankind to divine perfection and covenant fellowship. We have to understand that when we gave our lives to the Lord Jesus, we were made perfect. Sin will always bring about separation from the Lord and over time can bring about sickness, disease, pain, and soul wounds. Sin can be an open door and give legal ground for generational curses, disease, curses, sickness, etc. to exist in our lives. Physical death came through sin and disobedience through the first family (Adam and Eve).

Christ redeemed us from Adam's curse when He died on the cross for our sins and took the penalty of death on our behalf. We must understand that divine healing became one of the hallmarks of Christ's redemptive package through salvation and death on the cross. Spiritual death came through

Adam's disobedience and transgression, which relinquished our God-given right to have dominion on the earth. Jesus reconnects us into right fellowship with the Father. With divine healing, Jesus, throughout the Gospels, sent out His 12 apostles to preach the Good News and giving them authority to heal the sick (see Luke 9:1-2).

DIVINE HEALING IS BIBLICAL

There are cessationist views and schools of thought that believe healing ceased along with the gift of tongues and does not exist today as it did in the early church. I strongly disagree with that view, because after Jesus' resurrection and ascension, the apostles continued healing. There are many accounts in the Book of Acts where John, Peter, and Paul healed people (see Acts 5:12-16; 19:12; 28:8-9). We know that God is still *the Lord who heals you* (Exodus 15:26). God loves His people! He has not lost His power and ability to heal those who are in need.

Divine healing comes through a direct intervention by God in response to prayer, fasting, and confession by faith in His Word. I believe it is the Christian believers' inheritance to receive their divine healing, which belongs to them. Furthermore, we should know as believers that it's our right to be healed, delivered, and whole. Ignorance is one thing that the devil takes advantage of when believers do not know their spiritual and legal rights as children of God.

The definition of "legal right," defined according to Free Dictionary.com, is "an abstract idea of that which is due to a person or government body by law or tradition or nature." Think about what a legal right is: it denotes "a moral or legal entitlement to possess or by obtaining something or to act in a certain manner." When believers know their legal rights, especially pertaining to divine healing, they will approach any situation boldly. I believe that speaking the word of healing takes on a different aspect when we know who we are and our authority in Christ. Death and life is lodged in the power of our tongues.

The Bible is loaded throughout the Old and New Testaments with the supernatural nature and intervention of God and Him working through in

Jesus' ministry. Ignorance will hold us hostage of our spiritual legal rights. The enemy is known to be the accuser of the brethren, deceiver, father of lies, thief, trespasser, and more. I am reminded of an intruder who breaks unlawfully into someone's home. We must understand that the enemy is an adversary. The word "adversary" in the Greek is *antidikos* (Strong's G476), which means an opponent in a lawsuit or suit of law. The word *antidikos* comes from the root words: "anti" means against and the word *dikos*, which means "legal rights."

In other words, the devil is after your spiritual legal rights. The devil is the accuser of the brethren, he hopes you will walk in ignorance of your legal rights as a believer and keep you deceived—then he has the upper hand. We must not yield our legal rights to the enemy but rather wield the Word of God that is truth to remove the blinders. The enemy wants you to be ignorant and wants to keep you deceived from knowing who you are and what you are called to possess.

Yet not everything is a spiritual warfare battle or attack. There are also civil spiritual battles that need to be addressed in the Courts of Heaven. Allow the Holy Spirit to become the Special Counsel to help you fight and win spiritual civil battles against you. Through Jesus, He becomes our Advocate who handles all of our legal affairs, which have all been ultimately pardoned through the finished work of the cross.

As you are confronting the trespasser while notifying the authorities, it may be hard for anyone to believe that you are serious about evicting the intruder. But you will command him to leave so as to protect yourself, your family, and loved ones. If a person physically or sexually violates you, it is called rape, molestation, or sexual assault, depending on the degree of the situation. Your personal space is invaded illegally. On the other hand, anything consented to or permitted by you becomes legal, because you have given someone authority over your space and rights. The enemy wants to violate those who are ignorant of their legal rights in Christ Jesus. It is the intent of the enemy to afflict and inflict sickness, disease, and pain.

The enemy imposes unwelcomed evil upon God's people—and it is your divine legal right to use the power of the spoken Word of God to counteract his unlawful act. You have been given legal rights to resist the devil and he will flee (see James 4:7). Whenever the enemy comes to invade your personal space, know that you can activate an executive order of God's Word to remove it. United States President Donald Trump, in his first 100 days in office, signed many Executive Orders to be enforced immediately. These executive orders are like edicts or official decrees of action and intent to establish later law changes. Likewise, you have to speak life to your situation, while speaking death to the curse that the enemy tries to attach to you.

HEALING WORD PROPHETICALLY SENT

Psalm 107:20 says, *"He sent out His word and healed them, and delivered them from their destructions."*

I love this Scripture verse because it is clear that the word of healing was sent. In other words, when the Word of God is released, it carries healing power to bring deliverance. The word "deliverance" also means to rescue. When the enemy tries to plague your body with any sickness or disease, you have to send the Word of God by speaking the Word of God. The Word of God will heal and rescue whoever is distressed. In addition, the Word of God possesses resurrection power and it can serve as a preventative agent against sickness. When the spoken Word of God is sent, it will heal and rescue those in the pit and snatch them from the door of death, the grave, and imminent destructions.

Moreover, if we knew no sin, we should know no sickness. The weakness of the body is the effect of sickness and a weak immune system. We can prophesy a person's healing and the word sent will deliver what it was sent to do. When the Word of God is unleashed, it will not return unto God unfulfilled or void, it will accomplish what it was sent to do (see Psalm 55:11). The word spoken carries a prophetic element for it to be fulfilled. There are times in ministry when I was not physically able to get close enough to lay my hands on people who needed healing. Therefore, I just spoke the prophetic word of healing and they received it by faith and were healed.

The Word of God spoken over our lives serves as an anti-inflammatory, antibiotic, and antibodies to fight off spiritual and physical bacteria and sickness. We have to know that it is the will of our Father God to heal all who are stricken by sickness and disease. In addition, we have to understand with assurance that divine healing is the manifestation of this wholeness in our bodies; and when we refer to the body, we include the mind as well. It is the heart of the Father not only to heal us physically, but mentally, emotionally, and spiritually too.

Some Christian believers would suggest that healing by the Father is something He "might do" because He is sovereign. The problem with that non-biblical view is that nowhere in the Word of God proves that notion. As born-again believers, it is our divine, legal right to receive healing. Jesus proves that point on the cross:

First Peter 2:24 says, *"who Himself bore our sins in His own body on the tree, that we, having died to sins, might live for righteousness—by whose stripes you were healed."*

This Scripture proves that divine healing is the believer's right and the authority to receive it as well. Jesus Christ purchased it for us on the cross of Calvary and also destroyed the works of the devil. If the enemy can keep believers ignorant and silent, then he has control over them. God is always in the healing business. The word "heal" means to "cure or to make sound or whole."

There is a sound of healing or wholeness that comes through the Word of God when spoken with authority by those authorized. Healing is in our mouth. Healing not only impacts every aspect of our beings, but even our minds. We must know that sickness and disease is not limited to just the physical body, but the mind as well. There are many cases today of mental illness, disorders, sickness, and paralysis. A biblical case is of the man from Gergesenes who was demon possessed and mentally ill (see Matthew chapters 4 and 8).

In today's society there are people, and even Christians, who are suffering from extreme cases of bipolar disorder, depression, dementia, mental disorder/disability, and schizophrenia to name a few. Even believers are heavily medicated and go through much depression, oppression, trauma, and stress. Unfortunately, the enemy does not play fair and will attack our minds.

Divine healing spoken prophetically by faith will ease the dis-ease and will bring supernatural restoration and curing of the whole person—spirit, soul, and body.

Divine healing through the spoken Word of God takes place when born-again believers know their legal rights and appropriate the Word of God in his or her body members. What are we allowing to invade our spiritual and physical space that needs an eviction notice? What sickness and disease have we taken ownership of because we didn't see the result we were looking for immediately? What sickness have we hosted that needs to be ejected out? We must understand that our bodies are the temples of the Holy Spirit. It was made to host the Holy Spirit, not sickness, disease, demon spirits, or the spirit of infirmities.

YOUR BODY—A HEALING TEMPLE

First Corinthians 6:19 says, *"What know ye not that your body is the temple of the Holy Ghost which is in you, which ye have of God, and ye are not your own?*

The word translated "temple" is the Greek word *naos,* which means "… sacred edifice (or sanctuary)…" (Strong's G3485). The concept here is that our bodies are to be sacred places unto the Lord. We are spiritual priests unto God and kings on the earth. Sickness and disease has no place or room in our lives. We are righteous hosts of the glory of God and holy spiritual temples dedicated to bring glory to His name. We are Bethel in the earth! We become spiritual places where God through the Holy Spirit lives and dwells in our hearts.

It is time for people to nail an eviction notice on the door of death, sickness, and disease now! God dwelt in the Holy of Holies in the inner courts in the Old Testament; but in the New Covenant, the Lord makes our spirits and physical temple as His tabernacle. The Spirit of God quickens our mortal bodies and brings every cell and member of our body under subjection of His lordship.

The same spirit that raised Jesus from the dead is the same Spirit who lives in you (see Romans 8:11). God will heal those who need His healing. I must say that it is not that God "might" heal you when He feels like it—He knows that He will heal because He has the power. God is not sitting in Heaven blindfolded, randomly picking who He wants to heal. No! He wants to heal *all* in need. Believers must know their rights through God's Word, believe it by faith, and speak it boldly. Christ has taken away our sickness, so why are we living with it or bearing it? (See Matthew 8:17 NLT.) Speaking the word of healing is therapeutic and brings about the well-being of the whole person.

Believers should never get "comfortable" with their sickness or disease. Never settle for less than an abundant life, the one Jesus promised you. It is not your battle but the Lord's. Do not believe false teaching from leaders who say that it is God's will to teach you lesson with sickness. Do not be content and comfortable with your sickness—this is far from the truth of God's Word. Jesus paid it all and came to provide divine health, healing, and fitness through the atonement (see Romans 5:11,17). There are soul wounds and hurts that can affect our mental, physical, and spiritual health. The soul is the seat of our mind, will, and emotions. It is the place of our decisions. In addition, we have to be very cautious and clear on what we speak. We must be slow to speak and quick to hear (see James 1:19). Do not give in to the enemy's lie to receive what Jesus has already died for.

Luke 6:45 says, *"A good man out of the good treasure of his heart brings forth good; and an evil man out of the evil treasure of his heart brings forth evil. For out of the abundance of the heart his mouth speaks."*

My question: What are we speaking daily out of our mouths? What are we decreeing and confessing that does not belong to us? God desires His people to know the treasures of truth found in His Word concerning healing. Speaking words of healing will only come forth from a spring of revelation and truth of God's Word that He desires for His people. People only speak about the things that they put into their lives, whether it be sports, religion, money, soap operas, reality television, books, games, etc. As we learn the principle of God's Word and read about the countless healings, miracles, and supernatural intervention by God, our perspective will change.

The mouth is the only instrument and vehicle that God uses to get things accomplished. It is the only apparatus, prophetically, that God uses to bring about His divine plan and particular activity on the earth. I have seen the supernatural power of God work on my behalf as I spoke prophetically over those in need of healing.

SUPERNATURAL PREGNANCY

Back in 2015, I was preaching at a New Year's Eve service and I came across a young lady who asked me to pray for her. As I was praying for her, the Lord showed me her dire desire to give birth to a child. She wanted to have a baby and could not conceive a child because of birth implications from a previous childbearing. I began to prophesy to her physical womb, stomach area, and declare that she would give birth to a baby, a baby boy that God revealed to me.

A year later, I was ministering at a women's conference as a fill-in for a speaker who was unable to attend. The other conference speakers were all women, and I and my twin brother, Dr. Naim Collins, tag-team ministered the Word of God. After the message and during the offering time, I saw this same woman standing with her husband, and I noticed that she was not pregnant. God spoke to me to and He commanded me to prophesy to her again. The Lord revealed the gender of the baby and I prophesied by speaking that she would conceive.

The first time I had not addressed the issue why she couldn't conceive. This time I spoke the words of healing, life, and to her female organs to realign and function as God has ordained them to function. I rebuked the spirit of death, infertility and infirmities to her womb. Both the woman and her husband began to weep and fell out under the power of God. Two months later I received word that she was pregnant, and seven months later she gave birth to a healthy baby boy.

It was the power of the spoken word; but most importantly she believed the Word of God and received by faith her healing and spoke healing to herself. Because she believed the prophetic word of God concerning what was in her heart, her faith increased to believe the impossible; and like Hannah, she conceived what was in the abundance of her heart (mind).

My point is—what we harbor we conceive or give birth to. *Think healing, speak healing, and conceive your healing.* Get ready to speak the impossible and make it possible.

CHAPTER 5

Commanding and Confessing Your Healing

And I will give you the keys of the Kingdom of Heaven. Whatever you forbid on earth will be forbidden in heaven, and whatever you permit on earth will be permitted in heaven (Matthew 16:19 NLT).

God has given His people the keys of the Kingdom of Heaven. There is a Power Source who lives within each and every Spirit-filled believer—the Holy Spirit. We have the ability to command our day through prayer and prophetic decrees of God's Word. In addition, we can command our healing as well.

I had to come to an understanding of the purpose of what we possess. We can possess our healing through the present truth of what the Father says we can possess. For example, if you purchase your home or car, you are the owner of that home and car. You are now given the deeds to the home and title to the car. Moreover, you are responsible for the overall care of that vehicle and estate. The home is part of your assets, and you are given the keys of access to the home and car.

Furthermore, you have the authority and right to do what you want to do with those two assets because you are the owner. The keys to the home and car represent authority. No one without the keys have the access; and if they forcefully break into your home or car, they are one, breaking the law, and two, they are trespassers, thieves, and burglars. The intruders are unauthorized and haven't been given access permission and legal authority to enter. If you lose your own keys and have to break in, and the authorities are called, you will have to prove that you are the home and car owner. The car title, home deed and keys of access is proof of ownership.

HEAVEN—GOD'S COMMAND CENTER

We can see how imperative it is to have legal rights and authority. God has released divine Holy Spirit power and authority and given the keys of access to His children. We have the ability to possess our healing and command it as well. If someone breaks into your home, you do not ask them to leave, you command them to. Matthew 16:19 outlines the authority that the believer possesses. There is a command center in Heaven that we can tap into via the Holy Spirit. We communicate what Heaven is declaring! From the command center in Heaven, through faith we hear what the Lord is speaking to us through the Holy Spirit and His Word.

The Spirit-filled believer possesses the ability to bind and loose, permit and prohibit, arrest and release. Heaven will back you up as you flow with the Spirit of God. We can command our healing through the spoken word. We can prophesy and speak things into existence. We not only speak things into being through the words of faith, but we can rebuke tempest things that abruptly interrupt our lives. Jesus was on the boat asleep, a sudden storm came out of nowhere, and the disciples were afraid for their lives. Jesus discerns the motive and intent of the storm and spoke to the winds and the waters and His command was obeyed.

What are we speaking a word of calmness to and rebuking what is contrary to our purpose and destiny? Be like Jesus and speak to any life-threatening situation like the storm that came forth and command, "Peace, be still" in Jesus' name. I come to say to you prophetically, "Peace, be still, peace in your mind and heart concerning this sudden illness or long-term sickness, that fear of death is broken; and I decree that you will not be like the fearful disciples, but you will rest in the words of Jesus that calms every storm and healed every broken heart and sickness. BE HEALED in Jesus' name. Rest to recover!"

Words have power! When I was a youth, there was a familiar saying, "Sticks and stones may break my bones but words will never hurt me." Stick and stones can break bones, but I beg to differ with the rest of that saying. Words can harm a person, mentally and psychologically. Words have the capacity to hurt feelings, create wars, curses, and even bring about sickness, disease, and emotional pain.

In the natural realm, words can hurt or damage people's feelings. However, in the spiritual realm, words are containers of power that can change your life, alter your destiny, direct your future, and permit you to get your priorities in order with God's will. Words can carry God's supernatural power to heal your body, bring financial breakthrough blessings, and change any circumstance and situation instantly. Words carry the potency of bringing the prophetic promises of the Lord from the spiritual realm into the natural realm.

God has not created you to be sick for the rest of your life. It is not the will of the Lord for you to be saved, Spirit-filled, and sick at the same time. Break every fear, doubt, and personal reservation concerning your healing breakthrough. Oftentimes, we are waiting for the pastor, prophet, or healing evangelist who flew to our city to touch and pray for us to receive our healing. However, it will be *your faith* that will make you whole.

It is completely fine at times to find others to touch and agree in faith with you to receive your breakthrough. But in the meantime, what will you do, for example, if you are faced with an intruder who just broke into your home? While waiting for police to come, you are faced with doing something immediately. You may have to defend yourself by warding off the intruder until help arrives. I believe in self-healing, and I believe it can happen through commanding our bodies to function, operate, and work as God has created it to perform.

AUTHORITY OVER ALL THE POWER OF THE ENEMY

We must place a demand on the promises on God's Word. Healing is something we have to command and own for ourselves. Knowing that we have commanding power, it is clear to understand biblically what the authority and power has been given to us. Jesus emphatically stated in Luke 10:19:

Behold, I give you the authority to trample on serpents and scorpions, and over all the power of the enemy, and nothing shall by any means hurt you.

This Scripture verse in Luke 10 reveals God's original intent as it pertains to authority and power in the life of the believer. Jesus said we have power over *all the power of the enemy!* This means *all* and *any* works of the enemy, whether its sickness, disease, demons spirits, infirmities, etc. Jesus did not give us power to sit on the sideline and allow the enemy to short cut our healing and breakthrough. Jesus gave us power to do something with it. We possess the same power.

The ultimate Commander in Chief—Jesus Christ—has released delegated authority and power to you—the believer. He purposed for you to possess power and authority over the enemy. That may also mean through the power of your commands.

As we talk about authority and power, let's look at the New Testament definition. The first word translated "power" in Luke 10:19 is the Greek word *exousia* (Strong's G1849). That word basically means the "power of choice, freedom of action, right to act or power of authority." The Lord has given you *exousia* authority, which is like police officers who have been given the power of authority by the right of their badge to make an official arrest. Police officers have been given the right to act, or legal authority, to do the job. The badge is the *exousia,* which is the symbol that displays the officers' ability to exercise authority and legal actions to do what they are called and positioned to do. The gun without the badge doesn't mean anything, because the badge is what represents the sworn oath for public service.

A badge is the legal authorization given to an officer that is coded and has a specific identification number. The number is the officer's number, which links him or her back to the central command, station, authorized agency, or government that the officer represents. The badge number is connected to who they are and who authorized them. Moreover, a gun does not make an officer official; anyone can have a gun, the badge is what identifies and authorizes the officer to use his or her authority and a weapon. As a born-again, Spirit-filled believer, Jesus has given you *exousia* power to trample on anything contrary to His Word, and against you spiritually.

God has made us spiritual enforcers to bind and loose, trample upon anything that is not in the will of God. We are like officers given a badge of access and legal delegated authority to make commands that will bring results. Authority is our heavenly badge, seal, signet, and symbol that represent the government of God through the power (*exousia*) of the Holy Spirit. Jesus is the only authority, and everything bows and submits and confesses to Him (see Philippians 2:10-11).

Do not allow the enemy to tread upon you like a doormat—take up your bed and walk in your authority and healing. The second word translated "power" in Luke 10:19 is used to describe satan's ability. The word "power" referring to satan's ability is the Greek word *dunamis* (or *dynamis*), which means "ability, strength, force" (Strong's G1411). Let me be very clear here, the devil may have power (*dunamis*), but God has given you authority. Not only has God given you authority, but authority over *all* the limited ability (power) of the enemy!

SPIRITUAL LEGAL AUTHORITY AND RIGHTS

For example, a person may have a gun as the police do, but the police have authority and the right to carry a weapon because of the badge and *exousia* that has been given to him or her. The officer can make an official arrest of a person who is carrying a concealed gun that does not have a license to carry a weapon. The officer has the authority over the person who is not an officer with a badge who is carrying a deadly weapon. We have legal authority to command healing over any demonic opposition. The authority that Jesus has given you means that you have been given legal control, access and the right—and He is the only one who can delegate it to you.

In other words, Jesus has given you commanding authority over all the works of the enemy and He supports, backs, and reinforces you. A gun is a form of power, which can bring great harm if used; therefore, it represents *dunamis* (*dynamis*). As I stated, a criminal may carry a gun as can someone who is licensed to carry, but that does not mean anything compared to an officer with a badge who is authorized to enforce the law and make an arrest.

Likewise, demon spirits have power to do much harm to people with sickness and disease, but only the born-again, Spirit-filled, blood-washed believer has been authorized spiritually to command sickness, demon spirits, and the like to go away in Jesus' name. Every command spoken in Jesus' name is the spiritual authority that backs the believer.

John 1:12 (NIV) says, *"Yet to all who did receive him, to those who believed in his name, he gave the right to become children of God."*

It is God's desire for His people to take possession of what He has given them while knowing their spiritual rights. Commanding your healing by the Word of God will bring about results—if you believe. I believe it is not the Word of God that is the problem, it's our faith to believe what the Word of God says we can possess. The Word of God is true, and it works every time—if we allow it to work. We have to take God at His Word. In other words, we have to possess God's Word and use it for our benefit.

The Word of God is the key, and the Holy Spirit is the compass for healthy, prosperous, and righteous living. Debt, sickness, disease, and demon-free living! We have to know that Jesus' authority lives in us. It is not just any authority in us, it's the only authority in Jesus that is in us. The Bible says that, *"He who is in you is greater than he who is in the world"* (1 John 4:4).

HOSTING THE HEALING POWER

Sickness and disease has no rental space or place in our physical temples, our bodies. God did not create our bodies to become hosts for demons, sickness, disease, or pain. Our bodies are to be hosts of His presence, power, healing, virtue, and authority. We are called to command, tread on sickness and disease, and drive out demon spirits. Everything has to be subject to you! Whatever you are faced with today, know that through prophetic confession, commands, and declaration of the Word of God, you will see things change for the better.

The kingdom of darkness only functions within the confines and parameters of God's law. If a Spirit-filled, born-again, blood-washed believer is afflicted and infected with sickness, the devil has broken the law and now you can activate your legal rights of eviction, healing through the *exousia* (authority) that God has given you to stop him. When the enemy violates the law by breaking it to afflict you with sickness, then you must rise up and take authority over it.

If you have yielded yourself to sin, which has opened the door to satan and given him legal right to afflict you, then you must repent to God, renounce the act of sin, and close every legal ground given to the enemy. Evict, sever, and shut any evil alliance or open door. Command your freedom with the authority and power of God that has been given to you. I notice in the ministry of Jesus that He never prayed for the sick. He commanded them to be healed. Not only did Jesus command people to be healed, He gave His apostles the same authority to heal. It is a command, so we must firmly have that truth fixed in our minds. It is in the name of Jesus that we command healing to take place and demons to leave.

NO MORE EXCUSES

We can command our healing by speaking to the infirmity, that the damaged part of our body will be healed, and the demon spirits to be evicted. For example, Jesus healed a lame and sick man at the pool of Bethesda. This sick man was sitting by the pool year after year, waiting for someone to make something happen for him. He made a lot of excuses in his ignorance of what he could do. This man had been sick and crippled for 38 years. Jesus, knowing the length of the man's condition, asked him, *"Do you want to be made whole?"* (John 5:6).

Jesus challenged the man's mentality and paradigm concerning his condition. In addition, Jesus was assessing the man's heart and motive. There are people who want to be healed and say that they believe God will heal them, but they really do not believe what they are saying. Jesus was addressing the matters of his heart and what was on his mind. The man's physical condition obviously proves to be different from what he really believes. Thirty-eight years is a very long time, and it is hard to believe that he wanted healing.

He may have wanted healing, but Jesus wanted him to change his mentality for the need to be healed. The sick man replied to Jesus' question, *"Sir,"* the invalid replied, *"I have no one to help me into the pool when the water is stirred. While I am trying to get in, someone else goes down ahead of me"* (see John 5:7 NIV). He said "trying" and made excuses for not getting to the place of healing. The word *Bethesda* in Hebrew means "house of mercy" (Strong's H1534). The Lord's house will become a place of mercy and healing. The house of the Lord becomes a healing pool that releases the mercy of the Lord and the supernatural, raw power of God through yielded vessels.

It is the place of mercy where God desires to bring His people. The Lord creates the supernatural. An angel will come in a certain season to stir the waters. The sick man was waiting for someone to help him into the "Jacuzzi." There are many blaming others for their condition, rather than taking ownership to receive what the Father wants to give them. He spent so many years waiting on others, just like many of God's people today are waiting for others to help, heal, and relieve them of their suffering.

I believe what you are waiting for is already inside you through the Holy Spirit who is the Helper! People blame others for their pain, sickness, disease, and suffering and why they are in the place or condition. God wants to remove the excuses so you can rise up and take up your own bed (condition). Jesus challenged the man's will power and decisions. The Bible says *"faith without works is dead"* (read James 2:14-26). That verse of Scripture does not say that faith without other people's faith is dead. We have to give faith work to do for it to come alive. We *have to employ our faith in order to see healing take place.* Jesus challenges the condition of our mind-set and makes us responsible for receiving our own healing breakthrough.

HEALING MIND-SET

We must understand that our healing is predicated on our mind-set and faith in God's Word to do what it can do. We have to exercise our will in order for faith to work. Before Jesus could address the man's physical condition, He addressed the man's will. Later, Jesus addresses his view concerning healing and the power of God by questioning him, *"Do you want to be made whole?"* In other words, Jesus wanted to confront the man's doubt. The man needed to be made *whole* not just have his physical condition healed. God desires us to be transformed by His Word and the power of His Word. The man needed to know the mind and heart of Jesus—that not only could he be healed, he needed to be whole. He needed to change his mind before his condition could change.

We cannot wait on others for our healing breakthrough or blame others for not receiving our breakthrough. We have to look within ourselves, take responsibility over our condition, and make the faith determination to rise up and walk by the Word of God. Jesus healed the sick man at the pool of Bethesda, He said, *"Rise, take up your bed and walk"* (John 5:8). In other words, Jesus commands his healing by causing him to make a decision and act on it by faith. Jesus never prayed for him, nor did Jesus put him into the water. Jesus challenged his faith and mind-set. You have to change your mind-set and believe the Word of healing. Your condition doesn't dictate your healing. Your faith dictates your condition and brings about your healing and deliverance. The man received his divine healing and followed the commands of Jesus and was strengthened and healed totally.

COMMAND YOUR CONDITION

Jesus' first command to the lame man was to "Rise." This is the Greek word *egeiro,* which basically means "arouse from the sleep of death" (Strong's G1453); in other words, the man needed to awaken from the dead. He was dead spiritually, emotionally, and even soon to be physically dead—he needed personal revival. Jesus' command was not based on the impotent, sick man's ability, it was based on the life-changing, life-altering, and life-giving antidote given to the man. The impotent man needed spiritual therapy that came through Jesus' command. He was in that condition so long that it might have been very difficult for him to even recondition himself to walk again. He had to visualize his healing through confronting his present condition with the present truth of healing. The man was looking for man's help, but he needed help through God's Word. The ability was not in man, but in the ability to obey Jesus' healing command.

In another of Jesus' healings, He commanded the man with the withered hand, *"Stretch out your hand,"* and when the man did, his hand was restored as whole (Matthew 12:13). Jesus' disciples followed His lead and example and spoke the same healing commands, as revealed in Acts 3:6 in the healing of the crippled man: *"Then Peter said, 'Silver and gold I do not have, but what I do have I give you: In the name of Jesus Christ of Nazareth, rise up and walk.'"* In the next verse we see that Peter, *"took him by the right hand and lifted him up, immediately his feet and ankle bones received strength"* (Acts 3:7). We can see that healing commands were not limited to Jesus; his apostles had the authority and power too—as do *you,* as well. God is speaking prophetically for you to *rise, take up your bed and walk!* Command your condition to comply with the Word of God!

Speak to your condition to obey you. After you finish this book, you will see God's supernatural power working in your life. The commands and confessions over the course of 90 days serve as preventative medication—as what you speak forth by faith will keep sickness away. As long as you keep yourself sin free! The Scripture go on to say that the healed man began walking and leaping, and giving praise to God after receiving his miracle by God through Peter.

God desires His people to put their faith into action! He will cause you to do unusual things by stretching out your hands to believe by faith to see things restored, or taking up your bed and walking into a normal, productive life again, or even rising up and walking to receive total healing breakthrough for others to witness and believe God for theirs.

CONFESSING YOUR HEALING BY FAITH

That if you confess with your mouth the Lord Jesus and believe in your heart that God raised Him from the dead, you will be saved (Romans 10:9).

Therefore confess your sins to each other and pray for each other so that you may be healed. The prayer of a righteous person is powerful and effective (James 5:16 NIV).

The Word of God makes clear that confession of sin is imperative to receiving healing. James 5:16 reveals that confessing sin while praying for each other brings healing. We must know that the prayer of a righteous person is effective, powerful, and brings results. In the Christian experience, confession and forgiveness is an integral part in receiving healing breakthrough by the Word of God. Confessing your faults, offenses and sins to each other as believers brings healing and restoration through the act of prayer. We will never receive the blessing of healing by rejecting what the Word of God reveals concerning healing.

Can sin be one of the reasons for sickness and disease? Yes! However, there is a common misconception and ideology that we often hear concerning healing breakthroughs—that sin will prevent the believer from being healed. This is not biblically supported or logically sound. I have personally heard from popular Christian leadership and well-respected public figures in the Church that teaches that the reason people are sick is because there is sin in their lives. This preconceived idea or misconception does not align with the Word of God concerning healing. Sin doesn't prevent healing to take place in our lives so to speak—unbelief does.

Whatever theological belief systems we hold must be biblically supported and based on the uncompromised Word of God. There is evidence in the Old Testament that sickness is related to sin. However, is there any basis that unconfessed sin could hinder healing? Or sin in a person's life is the reason why they are sick in the first place? No! Jesus was always around sinners and He touched, healed and communicated with them which offended the religious leaders of His day.

I believe that confessing your sins, faults and sins to each other according to Scripture brings healing. But having sin in ones' life doesn't automatically prevent healing from ever taking place and sickness being the only reason as a result of sin *per se*. In John 5:14, Jesus healed and delivered a person and then tells him not to sin anymore. In this instance, we see the man received his healing breakthrough while sin existed in his life. Jesus has been given power in Heaven and on earth to heal the sick and forgive sins.

James 5:15 says, *"And the prayer offered in faith will make the sick person well; the Lord will raise them up. If they have sinned, they will be forgiven."*

SICKNESS ORIGINATED FROM SIN

A person's belief system outside the true Word of God has no solid ground and leads to error or assumptions. A believer will never receive healing breakthrough and the blessings of God without knowing the Scriptures. Jesus declares in Matthew 22:29 (NIV), *"You are in error because you do not know the Scriptures or the power of God."* Not knowing the power of healing and what the Scriptures say concerning healing hinders or prevents someone from receiving healing, deliverance, or breakthrough.

Sickness is not a result primarily due to sin in a person's life. Jesus, in John's Gospel, deals with a situation of a man born blind, and His disciples asked if the man's blindness was a result of his parent's sin or his own sin (see John 9:2). During the first century, many people connected all sickness to sin or evil activities. However, we must understand the origin of sin and that it is important to keep in mind that all sickness originated from sin and is inherently demonic in essence due to evil. Sickness and evilness were not in the original plan, purpose, or intent of the Lord and His Word.

Jesus addresses His disciples' inquiry about the blind man, saying *"Neither this man nor his parents sinned, but that the works of God should be revealed in him"* (John 9:3). I love what Jesus declared—that the purpose of this man's blindness was not sin but an opportune time for God to manifest His power through the supernatural invention to bring Him glory. Jesus broke off the wrong mind-set of His disciples, the mind-set that in that society of superstition, pride, self-righteousness, and ignorance of the Scriptures.

Jesus counteracted their religious perception with the truth and works of God. In John 9, the blindness was not a result of sin, nor did it come from God. Jesus came to destroy the works of the devil, and sickness is included. All we know is that the works of God manifested in the man's blindness, which was an evil condition that needed the power of God to reverse. We have to understand that it is not a sin issue but a belief issue in knowing the power of God. Sin does not block someone's ability to receive healing, and sickness is not always due to sin.

Many things can cause someone to be sick, diseased, crippled, or demonized. Do not accept sickness in your life! There are people who are not receiving their breakthrough healing because they believe that it came through sin or that sin is working in their life. Blindness in this man was a work of the evil one that needed to be destroyed by Jesus.

CONFESS BY RELEASING

In Romans 10:9, the word "confess" is the Greek word *homologeo,* which means "to speak the same thing, to assent, accord, agree with" (Strong's G3670). Furthermore, it means "to confess by way of admitting self guilt of what one is accused of, the result of inward conviction." When we confess, we are declaring, opening by way of speaking out freely; such confession by deep conviction of agreeing with someone or something verbally. You may be wondering what confession has to do with healing.

I believe that confession with prayer being done openly and verbally has to do with everything. Prayer not only changes everything, but also changes everything about you. Confession releases guilt, shame, condemnation, and self-martyrdom. Confessing what the Bible declares has to come from a knowing, understanding, and coming into agreement with the truth of God's Word. A person only confesses what he or she believes in their heart (see Romans 10:9).

The Word of God is the final authority in the life of the Christian believer. The very fact that you are saved today and have your salvation is because you accepted Jesus into your heart, believe that He lived, died on the cross, was resurrected, and ascended into Heaven for you. By confessing that you were a sinner and asking Jesus to be Lord over your life was the best decision you could ever make. Confession was your salvation. To confess and believe is to come into full alignment and covenant agreement with the Word of God and present truth.

The enemy knows the power of confession. The judicial system understands the power of confession. The devil fights against the believer from confessing consistently and persistently the Word of God; he recognizes the power of confession and its positive results. Furthermore, once we comprehend where sickness comes from, then we can understand why we have been given power to get rid of it. God's Word clearly discloses that both sickness and death originated with sin and now are being expanded by satan (see Romans 5:12-21; Job 2:6-7).

All that was oppressed by the devil, Jesus healed (Acts 10:38). I am reminded of what Jesus says in John 5:14, *"See, you have been made well. Sin no more, lest a worse thing come upon you."* After Jesus heals those who are oppressed by demon spirits, He instructs them to sin no more, lest a worse thing come on them. Only when sin is removed totally out of humanity will there be no more sickness (see Revelation 21). The Word of God teaches us that forgiveness of sins and healing of the body go hand in hand like a glove. I believe that healing is just as easy to obtain and receive from the Lord as forgiveness of sins.

Christ took our sickness and pain, so suffering does not belong to you—the believer. Faith comes by hearing, and hearing by the Word of God. Just as you can confess your sins to be healed, you also can confess the Word of God that brings healing. Fill yourself with the appropriate Word of God.

SATAN, THE SEED SNATCHER

Oftentimes it is assumed that if the Lord heals someone, possessing the healing is automatic. This is not the case at all. By the grace of God the healing will manifest; and the things we receive from the Father, we should possess by faith while maintaining it by faith. It is the desire of the enemy to keep you sick, diseased, poor, weak, bound, and defeated. The purpose of the devil (the thief) is to steal, kill, and destroy; but Jesus came that you may live and have life to the fullest, or abundantly (see John 10:10). The nature of God is constructive, abundant, prosperous, and good health. The nature of satan is destructive, murderous, sickness, and thievery.

The mission of the enemy, who was the god (ruler) of this world system, is to destroy and oppose everything pertaining to God and everything that God represents, which includes you the child of God. Notice that after you receive your healing or powerful prophetic word, the enemy will try to take it away from you. The devil is the seed snatcher, destroyer, and stealer. He comes to destroy the harvest seeds that God has planted in your life and garden. The enemy comes like a pestilence to destroy what God has cultivated and established.

> Matthew 13:19: *"When anyone hears the word of the kingdom, and does not understand it, then the wicked one comes and snatches away what was sown in his heart...."*

> Mark 4:14-15 NIV: *The farmer sows the word. Some people are like seed along the path, where the word is sown. As soon as they hear it, Satan comes and takes away the word that was sown in* them.

> 1 Peter 5:8-9 NLT: *Stay alert! Watch out for your great enemy, the devil. He prowls around like a roaring lion, looking for someone to devour. 9 Stand firm against him, and be strong in your faith....*

Guard your heart from seed snatchers that will come to steal your healing seed of faith. If you don't have enough faith to believe for healing breakthrough, I suggest speaking boldly out loud the confessions of God's Word each day until you believe it in your heart to be God's truth. In other words, you must believe what you confess. The enemy will come to rob you of the prophetic promises over your life. When you receive your healing after confessing the Word of God, your symptoms, condition, and pain may reoccur, but don't believe your body, believe the Word of God. Just because you feel pain or the symptoms may occur that immediately bring fear into your mind, or you may believe that you really didn't get healed by God—this is far from the truth. Healing is good and the will of God, and it is the Lord who gives every good gift. You must recognize the strategy of the enemy and stand against him with faith in God.

REBUKE THE SYMPTOMS AND CONFESS YOUR HEALING

If symptoms return to you after confessing your healing and the Word of God through prayer, then return to the Word of God and find His promise to base your faith upon. I must say that we should not be moved by our symptoms but be moved by the Holy Spirit to remove the sickness from our bodies. It is the purpose of the enemy to rob you of your healing by putting doubt in your mind regarding healing, by causing your symptoms to return. Be aware also that doubt and unbelief from other people who are skeptical about your healing by the Lord can forfeit of your faith and your healing breakthrough. If you feel symptoms return, refuse to accept it. If you have received Jesus Christ as your Lord and Savior, you now have delegated legal authority to rebuke, denounce the devil, and command him to go. We must know that a symptoms is not a sickness or disease but a symptom can alert us that something is happening in our bodies.

The Bible clearly reveals that God wills to be the Healer of His people, meaning that He declares His willingness to heal all those who obey Him. Christ's works of healing were not to prove His divinity but to prove His sovereignty and purpose of fulfilling the will of the Father. *"Behold, I have come to do, Your will, O God"* (Hebrews 10:9). Jesus is the revelation of the will of God, and He healed all who came to Him, which means He will heal, deliver, and save those who come to Him.

Confessing God's healing promises is key to defeating doubt, unbelief, and any lie of the enemy. This book will help increase your faith to believe for your healing, miracle, and deliverance now. Receiving the Word, and receiving the benefits from the Word of God, comes by being diligent. We must not just hear the Word of God, we must be doers of the Word of God. In other words, knowing and reading the Word of God and healing is not enough—we must declare, proclaim, confess, and profess it by faith.

GOD'S SUPERNATURAL MEDICINE
AND SUPPLEMENT

My child, pay attention to what I say. Listen carefully to my words. Don't lose sight of them. Let them penetrate deep into your heart, for they bring life to those who find them, and healing to their whole body. Guard your heart above all else, for it determines the course of your life (Proverbs 4:20-23 NLT).

The word *"healing"* stood out to me in this passage from Proverbs 4. When you look up the word "health," it literally means "medicine." It is powerful to know that God's will provides medicine (health) to your body to bring about healing. God's Word is medicine also to our spirit, soul, and body. Take God's medicine today and be made whole. Reading the daily confessions and commands in Part Two of this book will cause you to meditate on the Scriptures provided, and you will start to feel better as your faith increases. The word "meditate" means, "to mutter to yourself."

As you feed your faith by speaking and confessing the Word of God daily, you are taking your daily medicine. The written Word of God is the substance the Holy Spirit uses to make the word come alive or living words that quickens living words that produce life, joy, and peace to nourish our flesh. Philippians 4:8 says to meditate or think continually about good things and not earthly or carnal things. Having good health is a blessing, and possessing your healing is great and marvelous. God's Word is activated only when we are willing to work it by faith.

Never confess defeat. Always remember what Psalm 103:1-3 (NLT) says:

Let all that I am praise the Lord; with my whole heart, I will praise his holy name. Let all that I am praise the Lord; may I never forget the good things he does for me. He forgives all my sins and heals all my diseases.

As you move on to Part Two, I encourage you to look up all the healing Scriptures in the Bible, read them aloud, and meditate on them. Refuse to compromise with doubt, fear, and unbelief. Confess your healing here and now! Faith always activates your divine healing!

90-Day
Devotional

and

Activation Confessions and Commands that Unleash

Healing

EXODUS 15:26 (NIV)

He said, "If you listen carefully to the voice of the Lord your God and do what is right in his eyes, if you pay attention to his commands and keep all his decrees, I will not bring on you any of the diseases I brought on the Egyptians, for I am the Lord, who heals you."

God Heals His Covenant People

Today is a new day my special one. Open your ears to hear what I will instruct by My Spirit. It is new insight and revelation that I want to reveal to you. Listen carefully to what is on My heart concerning you. It is my desire to open your eyes to the truth of My Word in regard to healing, miracles, deliverance, and personal wholeness. As you tune in to My whisper this day and follow My commandments given in private, I will reward you openly with favor and blessings.

My promises toward you are yes and amen. I will not have you bent out of shape over the little things. I will be your Source, and I will overshadow you with good things. I will not cause you to live in disease-stricken condition, nor will I allow your body to be plagued with infirmities. I come to rescue you from all your fears and give you a healthy result that will extend your life. I will not cause your body and mind to be contaminated as those who live in darkness. You are in the light of My glory, and you shall be relieved from all your pain. I am a God of covenant, and I keep My promises spoken over you. I delight to see you arise and shine in the power of My glory.

SCRIPTURES

Proverbs 8:33; Isaiah 60; Acts 17:11; 2 Corinthians 1:20

HEALING PRAYER

Father God, thank You for healing me each day from things that I face daily. Keep me in Your perfect will. Open my eyes to the truth and allow me to gaze at what You desire me to focus on. When I am distracted, align me to the truth that will liberate and heal me. I want Your decrees to be what I live. As Your covenant keeper, allow me to be a good steward over my destiny. In Jesus' name, amen.

HEALING CONFESSIONS AND COMMANDS ACTIVATION

I CONFESS AND COMMAND that I am not conformed to this world, but I am transformed by the renewing of my mind. By this personal transformation, I prove what is the good, acceptable, and perfect will of God for my life (Romans 12:2).

I CONFESS that by Jesus' stripes, I am totally healed physically, mentally, and emotionally (Isaiah 53:3, 1 Peter 2:24).

I CONFESS that Jesus took all sickness and infirmities upon Himself for me on Calvary's cross (Matthew 8:17).

I CONFESS that Jesus Christ is the same yesterday, today, and forever in my life daily (Hebrews 13:8).

I CONFESS AND COMMAND that the law of the Spirit of life in Christ Jesus has set me free from the legalistic law of sin and death (Romans 8:2).

I CONFESS that the Spirit of Him who raised Jesus Christ from the dead lives inside me; He who raised Christ Jesus from the dead is giving me life and healing daily to my mortal body by His Spirit who lives in me (Romans 8:11).

I CONFESS AND COMMAND that by the mercies of God, I will present my body daily as a living and holy sacrifice, acceptable to God, which is my spiritual service of worship (Romans 12:1).

DAY 2

Exodus 23:25 (NIV)

*Worship the Lord your God, and his blessing will be on your
food and water. I will take away sickness from among you.*

God Takes Away the Pain

I know each day has its own problems, and the aches and pains are sometimes unbearable. My child, know that I do understand what it is like to
go through agony that strips you of your inner strength, peace, and physical
power. My Son Jesus endured the cross at Calvary and laid down His life on
a tree for the sins of the world. He can relate to you not having the physical
capacity to move on. He felt abandoned, betrayed by those He loved the most
and by His very own, ridiculed, persecuted, and rejected.

I have seen your afflictions, distress, and trials. I have come to take away
those inner aches, sickness, hurts, and feelings that remind you each day
when you are trying to press on. You don't have to own what you are experiencing in your body, mind, and spirit. I come to soothe your inner most
wounds and bring healing power to those scared places of the soul. Know
that I will be your spiritual nourishment that will replenish, revive, and
restore you to wholeness. Focus not on the pain, but focus on the power
within you by the Holy Spirit to take away every sickness, disease, pain,
and infirmity.

SCRIPTURES

Exodus 3:7; Hebrews 12:2; Hosea 6:2

79

HEALING PRAYER

Father, You heard my cry and You have seen my tears. Thanks for responding and coming to my aid. When I am weak, I am made strong in You. My trust is anchored in You. I will hold on to the promises of Your healing Word and will not let them out of my sight. You heal the broken heart and set at liberty the bound. I know that I am free from the pain, and no sickness will live in me. In Jesus' name, amen.

HEALING CONFESSIONS AND COMMANDS ACTIVATION

I CONFESS I have been purchased with a price, the precious blood of Jesus Christ; therefore I glorify God in my body and in my spirit, which are God's (1 Corinthians 6:20).

I CONFESS AND COMMAND that I will prosper and walk in divine health as my soul will prosper through the Word of God over my life daily (3 John 2).

I CONFESS AND COMMAND that the healing fire of God will burn out sickness, disease, illness, bacteria, and the spirit of infirmity that would operate in any part of my body, in Jesus' name.

I CONFESS that at the cross Jesus healed all diseases; therefore, my youth is renewed like the eagle's, in Your name (Psalm 103:3,5).

I CONFESS AND COMMAND that I will live and not die, and proclaim the Word of God; the Lord is my present strength, He has risen over me with healing in His wings. Therefore, no sickness or plague can remain in or come near my body (Psalm 91:10; 118:17; Psalm 27:1; Malachi 4:2).

I CONFESS AND COMMAND that I am fearfully and wonderfully created by the Lord and I command my body to operate and function in the way that He originally designed it to function. I forbid any malfunctions, breakdowns, and destruction in Jesus' name (Psalm 139:14).

I CONFESS AND COMMAND that there is nothing in my spirit, soul, or body that is not of You and that there is a spiritual detox, purging, and cleansing by Your Spirit and Word, in Jesus' name.

DAY 3

DEUTERONOMY 34:7 (NIV)

Moses was a hundred and twenty years old when he
died, yet his eyes were not weak nor his strength gone.

God Renews Strength and Vision

Good day, My child. I come to renew your strength and sharpen your ability to see. Know that I come to awaken the dream and destiny that I have orchestrated for you before the foundations of the world. It is not My will for your life to live in a realm of defeat and complacency. I didn't make you to be indestructible, but created you to live in a realm of possibilities. Your vision will not die regardless what life or your health conditions says. It is My heartbeat to infuse your faith today to see yourself coming out and overcoming every health issue.

You are an overcomer in Christ. You were not created to live in normalcy but to be a mover and a shaker in your generation. Yes, I am aware that you are growing fast and getting older day by day. With time there is wisdom and experience that is adopted. As you have ears to hear what the Spirit is saying to you daily, you will arise to the occasion and settle the inner turmoil of uneasiness that comes to frustrate you. I will restore the years you lost and renew your strength as the days of your youth. You will not die prematurely but arise as one with great vision, like an eagle, to see your purpose clearly.

SCRIPTURES

Genesis 37:5-10; I King 3:3-15; Isaiah 40:31;
Joel 2:25; Mark 4:9; John 16:33

HEALING PRAYER

Thank You, Father, for giving me the ability by the Holy Spirit to see my self-worth and value. It is my heart's desire to grow in grace and in the knowledge of Your dear Son, Jesus. I want to be used for Your glory. Allow me to focus on what You have for me and only me. Give me the supernatural power to accomplish Your will in my life with a God-ease. Sharpen my spiritual lenses that I may see as You see my life. In Jesus' name, amen.

HEALING CONFESSIONS AND COMMANDS ACTIVATION

I CONFESS that Jesus Christ is the Lord over my life. Sickness and disease has no place and power over me. I am forgiven and free from sin, shame, and guilt. I am dead to sin and alive unto righteousness (Colossians 1:21-22).

I CONFESS that I am free from unforgiveness, strife, bitterness, resentment, and malice. I forgive others as Christ has forgiven me, for the love of God is shed abroad in my heart by the Holy Spirit (Matthew 6:12; Romans 5:5).

I CONFESS that Jesus Christ has taken all my sickness, disease, and illnesses and carried my pain. Therefore, I give no place and power to sickness or pain in my life and body. For God sent His healing Word and healed me totally (Psalm 107:20).

I CONFESS that the Father causes me to reign over and become an overcomer through His Word. I overcome the world, the flesh, and the devil by the blood of the Lamb; and the word of my testimony causes me to triumph (1 John 4:4; Revelation 12:11).

I CONFESS AND COMMAND over my life that I have been given abundant life in Christ and I receive life through His Word, and it flows like a river to every organ of my body bringing healing and health (John 6:63; 10:10).

82

2 CHRONICLES 7:14 (NIV)

If my people, who are called by my name, will humble themselves and pray and seek my face and turn from their wicked ways, then will I hear from heaven and will forgive their sin and will heal their land.

God Responds to the Humble

Don't allow pride to become a stumbling block that will cripple you from moving forward in life. The enemy has a plan to shortcut your destiny before you ever get started. Pride is the enemy of your destiny and even I resist the haughty heart. Humility will release the treasures of Heaven and cause you to walk in liberty and divine blessings. Seek My face daily, so that I can answer your most difficult problems. I am here to resolve them, and together we will solve them.

Turn from evil doers and keep yourself clear on a pathway of destiny. You can call upon Me anytime and I will not send you to voicemail or forward your prayer petition to a pending status. I will get right on it. My ears are open to your voice, and I desire to open the heavens over you to heal you and those you ask Me to heal, touch, and bless. Pray for Me to heal your family, city, community, nation, and I will bring sudden revival as they turn their hearts over to Me. I turn a deaf ear to the prideful, but to the humble I will listen and act on their behalf.

SCRIPTURES

Deuteronomy 28:12; Proverbs 3:7, 28:9, 16:8; Matthew 16:23

HEALING PRAYER

Father, I humble myself daily before Your presence, coming for answers. I repent if I have done wrong in Your sight. Forgive me for anything I have done, spoken unknowingly and knowingly. I want to walk under an open heaven. I want to be totally healed and set free from life's strongholds. Wash me and make me whole so I will walk in peace, joy, and righteousness daily in the Holy Spirit. In Jesus' name, amen.

HEALING CONFESSIONS AND COMMANDS ACTIVATION

I CONFESS that as God was with Moses in the days of old, so the Lord will be with me. My eyes are not dim; neither are my natural forces abated. I declare blessed are my eyes for they see and my ears for they hear (Deuteronomy 34:7).

I CONFESS AND COMMAND that no evil will befall me; neither shall any plague come near my dwelling. For Father, You have given Your angels charge over me. They keep me in all my ways. In Your pathway is life, healing, miracles, deliverance, great health, and there is no death (Psalm 91:10-11; Proverbs 12:28).

I CONFESS that Jesus Christ took all my infirmities and my sickness. Therefore, I refuse to permit sickness or disease to dominate or invade my body. The life of God flows within me bringing healing to every fiber of my being (Matthew 8:17; John 6:63).

I CONFESS AND COMMAND that I am redeemed from the curse according to Galatians 3:13. Life is flowing in my blood system and stream. It flows to every blood cell in my body, restoring life and perfect health, in Jesus' name (Mark 11:23; Luke 17:6).

I CONFESS AND COMMAND that the life of First Peter 2:24 is a spiritual and natural reality in my flesh, restoring every cell of my body.

2 CHRONICLES 16:12 (NIV)

*In the thirty-ninth year of his reign Asa was afflicted with a disease
in his feet. Though his disease was severe, even in his illness he
did not seek help from the Lord, but only from the physicians.*

God The Great Physician

I know you may not be feeling well at times, My beloved, physically and spiritually. I come to build and reconstruct those things that have depleted your energy, your faith. What has discouraged you that you cannot trust Me to do the impossible? Do not walk in a place of defeat, but walk in faith and victory. Know that I will remove that shame and blame that comes at times when you are weak. I will shift your focus to My promises in My Word. I am reconditioning your mind to think on those things above and not beneath.

I am sending My angels before you to make every crooked place straight and straighten out your walk with Me with truth. The enemy wants you to bring doubt, fear, unbelief, and anxiety to that what you cannot control. It is the strategy of the accuser of the believer to believe a negative report and diagnosis. Jesus is still a miracle worker and will heal every sickness and disease that plagues you. I know your body may be hurting, but reach up and receive your miracle breakthrough today. Renounce fear and pronounce faith that will release your healing today. Whose report will you believe? Jesus died that you may have life and more abundantly. I say live and be healed. Trust My report and believe that it contains the prescription you need to get better.

SCRIPTURES
Jeremiah 34:1; Isaiah 45:2; John 10:10

HEALING PRAYER

Father, I will not believe the report of the doctors; I believe the report of the Lord. You bring reassurance that everything will be ok. You have my best interest and will not leave me without answers. You hear me when I call. I will stand on the promise of Your Word. You send Your Word to heal me. You are my Primary Care Physician. You are my healing pill and daily antidote. In Jesus' name, amen.

HEALING CONFESSIONS AND COMMANDS ACTIVATION

I CONFESS AND COMMAND that I will present my body to the Lord, for it is the temple of the living God. He dwells in me and His life permeates my spirit, soul, and body so that I am filled with the fullness of God daily (Romans 12:1-2; John 14:20).

I CONFESS AND COMMAND that my body is the temple of the Holy Spirit. I make a demand on my body to release the right chemicals. My body I declare is in perfect chemical balance. My pancreas secretes the proper amount of insulin for life and health, in Jesus' name (1 Corinthians 6:19).

I CONFESS that Jesus is the Great Physician and He knows all my issues and problems. He will heal and care for me daily.

I CONFESS that my heavenly Father, through His Word, has imparted life into me. That life restores my body with every breath I breathe and every word I speak (John 6:63; Mark 11:23).

I CONFESS that whatever God has not planted or imparted in me dissolves and is rooted out of my body, in Jesus' name.

I CONFESS AND COMMAND that the healing virtue of the Lord is released as I trust and pursue healing daily.

I CONFESS AND COMMAND that I am healed by the power of the Holy Spirit and I am not bound to any sickness, disease, or disability, in Jesus' name.

PSALM 27:1 (NIV)

*The Lord is my light and my salvation—whom shall I fear? The
Lord is the stronghold of my life—of whom shall I be afraid?*

God A Stronghold When You Are Weak

Fear not, My love child. This is a day of flawless victory and perpetual breakthroughs. Whatever you have been facing that has defiled and restricted
you from advancing in Me, I will become a bulldozer and make clear the path
before you. It is My heart to see you well and in good health. Fear comes to
grip you from believing Me for the impossible. I have not given you a spirit of
fear, My child. Do not accept no for an answer or allow the negative results to
dictate or bully your faith. Silence the voice of doubt, sickness, pain, fear, and
death. You will not walk in the darkness.

For I have transferred you from the kingdom of darkness into My Kingdom light. I will be a pillar against the adversary who seeks to destroy your
spiritual house. My Holy Spirit will take residence in you and build a place
upon a sure and strong foundation. I am your Strongman and will evict
every evil spirit and spiritual rodent that migrates to that who I call Mine.
Do not be afraid but ARISE in the power of My might!

SCRIPTURES

*Mark 3:10; Luke 18:27; 2 Timothy 2:19; 1
Corinthians 3:11; Colossians 1:13*

HEALING PRAYER

You keep me from falling and crumbling. You are my strong tower that I run into and I am safe. Father, seal up the breached places and mend the gates that have been broken in my life. I am weak, but I know I am strong in you. Give me a way of escape when my salvation is on the line. Continue to be my Salvation and voice of hope. In Jesus' name, amen.

HEALING CONFESSIONS AND COMMANDS ACTIVATION

I CONFESS AND COMMAND that not every stronghold in my life will influence me life in a negative way, but that God will release healthy strongholds that will act has blockers to any sickness and disease, in Jesus' name.

I CONFESS AND COMMAND that I am healed by the Word of my mouth and overcome by the word of my testimony.

I CONFESS AND COMMAND that healing is my portion and that sickness and disease do not take ownership in my life or in those I love.

I CONFESS that Jesus' blood covers and protects me from any demonic plague and sickness that tries to invade my body, in Jesus' name.

I CONFESS AND COMMAND that the Word of healing over my life strengthens me daily and that nothing will hinder my speedy recovery.

I CONFESS that Your Word, Father, has become part of me. It is flowing in my bloodstream. It flows to every cell of my body, restoring and transforming my body. Your Word has become flesh; for You sent Your Word and healed me (James 1:21; Psalm 107:20; Proverbs 13:3).

PSALM 30:2 (NIV)

Lord my God, I called to you for help, and you healed me.

God Heals The Helpless

When you pray, My loyal one, I am always listening. Your voice is like music and a lovely melody to My ears. Do not think for a minute that you are bothering Me when you ask for personal things that can better you. I know it is difficult at times when losses and even unfortunate occurrences shake up things a bit in your life. I come to break every ungodly cycle and pattern that has opposed your breakthrough and healing. I am willing and able to heal you, forgive, relieve you, strengthen you, bless you, promote you, sustain you, love you, favor you, and honor you.

I am not in the business of leaving you alone, having to fend for yourself. It is the responsibility of a loving Father like Myself to protect and fight for those I call My own. You are My child and I do not like to see you in any condition that is not My will. When you are too weak to speak, know that your whisper for relief will signal Me to respond in a hurry. Call upon Me and I will rescue you in the time of need. Let healing be your portion today!

SCRIPTURES

Psalm 96:1; Isaiah 41:10; 1 John 5:14; Colossians 1:11

HEALING PRAYER

My God, You are a healer when I call for instant results. You said in Your Word that the prayers of the righteous avail much. I want to stay in right standing with You. I don't want to walk in ignorance but the truth, knowing that it is the truth that will make me free. I am confident that every time I call You, Father, You never let me down. In Jesus' name, amen.

HEALING CONFESSIONS AND COMMANDS ACTIVATION

I CONFESS AND COMMAND that my healing needs are met by the Lord Jesus Christ.

I CONFESS that Jesus is my Healing Agent and He is sending angels of healing to my aid and bedside.

I CONFESS that the Holy Spirit is releasing the healing rivers of life that will flow in my body and free me from any spirits of oppression and depression.

I CONFESS AND COMMAND that I am not my past nor do I look like what I have been through, in Jesus' name.

I CONFESS AND COMMAND that a supernatural recovery, accelerated healing, and the power of deliverance is my portion daily.

I CONFESS that Jesus is seated at the right hand of the Father making intercession on behalf of me, and I am being touched by His healing power and words from Heaven.

I CONFESS AND COMMAND that unforgiveness, strife, bitterness, guilt, and shame do not live in my sphere and life, in Jesus' name.

I CONFESS AND COMMAND that my mind, body, and soul belong to the Lord, and my spirit is redeemed and made alive in Christ.

PSALM 34:19 (NIV)
The righteous person may have many troubles, but
the Lord delivers him from them all.

God Scatters Trouble Makers

I know today, My child, may not be the best day for you. Sometimes your body is not agreeing with your faith and mind to overcome. There are times you are not feeling one hundred percent. People, places, and things can cloud your mind and overwhelm you. Constant negative vibes and energy does not make things better. The enemy likes to use vulnerable moments when you least expect and then he will throw his jabs. Weeping may come at times when you have had it, but know that I will bring joy in your mourning.

Startled at the moment of what just happened can cause you to lose sight of your purpose or even ask yourself if it is all worth it? My child, know that I will defend and defeat the instigators of trouble that come to frustrate your divine season. I will remove the trouble that seems to follow those who are on the right track. It is my intent to dispel and dismantle those who rise up against you. I will cause them to flee as you resist them. If I am before you, then who can be against you? You have nothing to worry about. I got your back!

SCRIPTURES

Romans 8:27-37; Luke 4:3; James 4:7

HEALING PRAYER

Trouble comes to break me down and break my stride in pursuing You, Father. I thank You for delivering me out of the hands of the wicked. My future is sure in You, and I trust that I will be better today than I was yesterday. The enemy comes in like a flood to drown me out, but You lift up a standard against him. You are my Lifeguard! Raise me up to be a faithful vessel for Your glory. In Jesus' name, amen.

HEALING CONFESSIONS AND COMMANDS ACTIVATION

I CONFESS that Jesus Christ bore the curse for me; therefore, I forbid growths and tumors to inhabit my body. The life of God within me dissolves growths and tumors, and my strength and health are restored completely (Matthew 16:19; Mark 11:13; John 14:13).

I CONFESS that Jesus will remove all fear, anxiety, stress, depression, oppression, confusion, and anything that will affect my mind, body, and soul in a negative way, in Jesus' name.

I CONFESS AND COMMAND that I am the righteousness of Christ and sickness and disease has no room in my life; I evict them all, in Jesus' name.

I CONFESS AND COMMAND that my faith is increased daily as God is restoring my health, renewing my mind, and rebuilding my body.

I CONFESS AND COMMAND that bad news from doctors and reports will not influence my emotions in a negative way, but help me to pray and seek better solutions for recovery and healing.

I CONFESS AND COMMAND that I will be a sign, wonder, and a miracle for others to be blessed.

I CONFESS AND COMMAND that I am marked with supernatural healing powers by the Holy Spirit to lay hands on the sick and they shall recover and speak to any mountain by faith and it will move and obey me, in Jesus' name.

PSALM 91:9-10 (NLT)
*If you make the Lord your refuge, if you
make the Most High your shelter,
no evil will conquer you; no plague will come near your home.*

God A Dwelling Place for Safety

Through the Holy Spirit, I dwell in You. As I am One with My Son Jesus, I desire to be one with you daily. Come into My presence and find safety from all your troubles. I know you may not be feeling well at times, but in My presence you will receive the healing touch that will break the lies that the evil one sends to shake your faith. Know that as you commune with Me, that My glory will be evident in and through you. I will come and tabernacle with you. Allow your heart to be a sanctuary of love that I can seek and rest in.

I search far and near looking for a heart that will be a dwelling place where I can come down and live by My Spirit. Where I dwell, no thief or robber can break into. My child, I protect and guard that in which I dwell. Not only am I seated on My sovereign throne, but allow the altar of your heart to be a place where My Son Jesus can be seated and reign and rule. No sickness, disease, or infirmity will plague what I have called sacred and holy. You are the temple of the Holy Spirit and no harm will destroy or disrupt our tent of meeting. I am your Refuge and place of restoration.

Ezekiel 37:27; Psalm 91; 1 Corinthians
3:16; 2 Corinthians 6:16

HEALING PRAYER

Father, You are my hiding place. In Your presence, I feel peace and healing that surpasses all my understanding. Give me the clearance to build You a place where You can live and dwell in me. Remove any ungodly altars or idols of the heart that I have erected that are blocking my healing breakthrough. I confess that I am made whole in You. In Jesus' name, amen.

HEALING CONFESSIONS AND COMMANDS ACTIVATION

I CONFESS that in the presence of God there I will find healing and safety.

I CONFESS that in the presence of God I will find peace, joy, and rest.

I CONFESS AND COMMAND that I will not carry what has been on my past generation. I denounce and renounce all generational and hereditary curses, sicknesses, and diseases, in Jesus' name.

I CONFESS AND COMMAND that I am totally free from any generational curse and Jesus took on the curse for me and has liberated me from its impact.

I CONFESS that Jesus canceled every negative and demonic assignment against my health, mind, body, and soul. Therefore, I am healed in every way, and my life will prosper in the truth of God's Word over my life.

I CONFESS AND COMMAND that my life is hidden with Christ, my body is a sanctuary of the Holy Spirit, and sickness and disease will not take residence in me.

I CONFESS AND COMMAND that I will not be cut off prematurely, nor will I live in ignorance of God's Word; His truth will make me free daily, in Jesus' name.

PSALM 91:11 (NIV)
*For he will command his angels concerning
you to guard you in all your ways...*

God Sends Angelic Reinforcement

My dear one, I know when your back is against the wall and you are facing imminent decisions. I will give you the answers to unravel and solve. Stay on the course that I have set before you. It is the devil's plan to get you stuck in the mud of life, never having the traction needed to come out of it. Life can bombard you suddenly at times and you must juggle all the different trials. Do not drop the ball. I will assist you and ease the load. You are being tested! The enemy is threatened by your potential to be great in Christ. He only attacks those who can defeat him. Know, My child, that he is already defeated. I have angels on assignment ready to heal, restore, and bless you.

Give no room for the enemy through sin, unforgiveness, resentment, bitterness, offense, guilt, shame, and self-condemnation. I will ward off these demonic stigmas that attach to those who are faithful to the call. I will summon and send on your behalf My angelic army to fight your spiritual battle. Work with Me and not against Me. Trust Me in every detail of your life. Do not take ownership over any unnecessary burden or responsibility that I have not given you. The enemy wants to stress you out and overwhelm you to cause depression, sickness, immunity breakdown, and mental dysfunction. You will live and not die and declare the acts of your God.

SCRIPTURES
Psalm 91:11; Isaiah 65:24; Ephesians 4:27

HEALING PRAYER

I know that there is more with me than those that are against me. Father, when I need You, You are always readily available to deliver me. Thank You for caring for me so much that You send spiritual reinforcement as a sign that You hear my healing prayers and supplications. In Jesus' name, amen.

HEALING CONFESSIONS AND COMMANDS ACTIVATION

I CONFESS that God has assigned to my life warring and healing angels to protect, guard, form a fence around about me, and heal me.

I CONFESS AND COMMAND that what the enemy meant for bad, God is turning around and working it out for my good, in Jesus' name.

I CONFESS AND COMMAND that I am walking in the fruit of the Spirit and gifts of the Spirit. I renounce any work of the flesh and carnal thinking and break the spirit of unbelief, doubt, and fear.

I CONFESS AND COMMAND that every organ, cell, bone, tissue, and member of my body function in the perfection that God has created and ordained them to function. I forbid any malfunction in my body, in Jesus Christ's name (Genesis 1:28,31).

I CONFESS that Father, Your Word would manifest in my body, causing abnormal growths to disappear. Arthritis is a thing of the past, sickness and disease is also, and healing is my reality now. I make a demand on my bones and joints to function properly, in Jesus' name (Matthew 17:20; Mark 11:23).

I CONFESS AND COMMAND that sickness must flee now, tumors cannot and will not exist, cancer will never plague my body, bones, skin, and blood cells because the Spirit of God is upon me and the Word of the Lord is within Me. Sickness, fear, and oppression as a result of a doctor's report have no power over me, my decisions, my mind, body, and soul—the Word of God has the final word, which is my confession (Mark 11:23).

PSALM 103:1-5 (NIV)

Praise the Lord, my soul; all my inmost being, praise his holy name.
Praise the Lord, my soul, and forget not all his benefits—who forgives
all your sins and heals all your diseases, who redeems your life from
the pit and crowns you with love and compassion, who satisfies your
desires with good things so that your youth is renewed like the eagle's.

God Renews Strength like an Eagle

I will deliver you from falling into the pit of sin and redirect your path to success. Continue to praise Me and exalt My name above everything. There are daily benefits that I desire to release to you for just being you. I call you My friend, and with any friendship there are expectations. I expect the best out of you. You were destined to be great and walk in a measure of favor that I will place upon you.

Know that I will heal all your diseases and restore the years that you may think have been wasted. Know, My child, that I will crown you with goodness. You will see renewed strength come upon you like an eagle that has come out of the molting season. I will restore new feathers that will give you new flight and allow you to soar beyond any personal obstacles that you may face. You shall mount up on wings as an eagle and you will accelerate swiftly in the Spirit.

SCRIPTURES

Proverbs 3:6; Isaiah 40:31; Psalm 121:3; James 2:23

HEALING PRAYER

Father, You know the areas that I face daily. I am weak in my body and need Your Holy Spirit virtue to recalibrate me and raise me up. I will praise You in the good times and even in the worse moments. You will nourishment me with Your love. In Jesus' name, amen.

HEALING CONFESSIONS AND COMMANDS ACTIVATION

I CONFESS AND COMMAND that my strength is being renewed daily like an eagle.

I CONFESS AND COMMAND that I will not be spiritually or physically malnourished, in Jesus' name.

I CONFESS that when I am weak, God is strong in me and that I have the spiritual protein that will restore my strength.

I CONFESS AND COMMAND today that I am stronger than I was yesterday, and I will not die but declare the wonderful works of the Lord.

I CONFESS AND COMMAND that sin will not be a hindrance or stronghold in my life; I turn over every sin to the Lord and I am forgiven of them.

I CONFESS AND COMMAND that I will walk by faith and not by sight, in Jesus' name.

I CONFESS AND COMMAND that healing and miracles are my portion, and I am claiming both by faith in Christ.

I CONFESS AND COMMAND that daily I attend to God's Word and that I will incline my ears to hear His prophetic words over me. I will not let them depart from my eyes. I will keep them in the midst of my heart, for they are life-changing and healing to all my flesh (Proverbs 4:20-22).

PSALM 107:20 (NIV)

He sent out his word and healed them; he rescued them from the grave.

God's Word A Healing Lifeguard

There are times when you may feel like the currents and waters of life are getting above your head. You feel that you cannot stay afloat. Nevertheless, My child, stand on the buoyance of My Word and promises that will keep you from drowning. This is a time when I will send forth My Word to strengthen you; you will not lose your footing. Stand on My Word and watch yourself swim to the top with no resistance. The enemy desires to see you wiped out and feel numb to the conditions that come to you.

I will resuscitate you by My Holy Spirit when you have taken your last breath. For too long you have been holding your breath under the water of a troubled life. I am your Lifeguard and will heal you when you are sick and will come to you when you are exhausted. Confess My Word of healing that will be sent to rescue you and revive you when you call upon My name. This is not the season to become fatigued or lose sight of what I have in store for you. I know it is hard to feel the earth under your feet sometimes, but My promise will be your island, beach, and boardwalk to rest and bask in My presence.

SCRIPTURES

Isaiah 40:8; Proverbs 119

HEALING PRAYER

Your Word spoken becomes a guiding lamp upon my feet and light upon my path. When I am so drained, Father, You energy me. Your Word becomes a safety net for me to hold on to when I have gone too deep in worry. Keep me afloat in Your presence. In Jesus' name, amen.

HEALING CONFESSIONS AND COMMANDS ACTIVATION

I CONFESS that Jesus is my Lifeguard; and when I am drowning in sin, He forgives me and revives me to right standing in Him.

I CONFESS that God's healing power by the Holy Spirit lives and abides in me.

I CONFESS AND COMMAND that I will not receive a false report or negative word over my health, mind, body, or soul, in Jesus' name.

I CONFESS AND COMMAND that I am focused on the promises of the Lord for my life and they are yes and amen.

I CONFESS AND COMMAND that I will not walk in sickness and disease, but healing and deliverance.

I CONFESS AND COMMAND that I have a strong, beating heart. My heart beats with the rhythm of life.

I CONFESS AND COMMAND that Jesus' blood flows to every cell of my body, restoring life and health abundantly (Proverbs 12:14; 14:30).

DAY 13

I will not die but live, and will proclaim what the Lord has done.

God's Word Redeems, Restores, and Resurrects

ook at the stars, moon, clouds, waters, and those things that I have created that represent My Master touch. These things are just examples of My creative ability and craftsmanship. You are one of My greatest creations. I called humanity into being and you were destined to rule the earth with dominion that I have given to you in your DNA. You were created to live a life that is righteous, holy, and in peace. The enemy wants to kill, steal, and destroy you and your prophetic destiny. Your healing is lodged in My healing touch. Sickness has no match against Me!

I will veto and overrule his plots and cause you to be restored to a place of authority in the Holy Spirit. My Word will come to redeem the years that you have lost sight of. I will restore what has been taken from you and destroyed. Know, My child, you shall not die but live to declare what My promises are concerning you. I shall resurrect you and cause you to not fall prey to sickness, illness, disease, pain, hurts, and things that will bring decay to you. This is your coming out party! Awake and get dressed. This is a new season and day for you.

SCRIPTURES

Genesis 1:1,26; Psalm 118:17; Joel 2:25

HEALING PRAYER

Father, thank You for caring for me enough to see my worth when I don't feel worthy. I am humble to be called Your child. Your Word over my life brings me out of the grave that life has already put me in. You deliver me out of the nailed coffin and allow me to live in total healing. In Jesus' name, amen.

HEALING CONFESSIONS AND COMMANDS ACTIVATION

I CONFESS that God's Word redeems, restores, and resurrects every lost, wasted, and dead thing in my life.

I CONFESS AND COMMAND that life belongs to Jesus and not the enemy of my life and destiny.

I CONFESS AND COMMAND that I am healed by the Word of God and have what the Word of God says I can possess.

I CONFESS AND COMMAND that my emotions are in order and I am sober by the Word of God that is my foundation.

I CONFESS that the Holy Spirit empowers, heals, delivers, equips, and activates what I desire to see happen in my life spiritually.

I CONFESS that God's Word is life-changing and that I am walking in personal revival, restoration, and transformation.

I CONFESS AND COMMAND that my life has a fresh start, and I am healed in my mind, body, and soul.

I CONFESS AND COMMAND that lung disease, pneumonia, fluid in the lungs, asthma, respiratory distress, shortness of breath, and lung cancer is cursed at the root, and I am totally healed, in Jesus' name.

Psalm 147:3 (NIV)
He heals the brokenhearted and binds up their wounds.

God Heals Wounds with Love

ood morning, My beloved. I see what you encounter daily. I also feel what you feel and hear what you have to listen to daily that does not bring joy, peace, and ease. I understand when your heart has been broken and there are times when you are faced with making important decisions. But know, My child, that I was right there watching and listening. Those decisions were not easy ones to make. When your heart felt like it had been shattered into a million pieces, unable to be put back together again, know that I have more than super glue—My unconditional love will seal up any wound or scar.

I will mend the broken places in your life and heal the wounds of the past that keep you obligated to them. Free yourself from any unhealthy relationship and anything that will hinder you from walking in total liberty and deliverance. Trust in Me with your whole heart and allow me to gather the damaged parts of your heart. I will gather the scattered pieces and fragments of your heart that were ripped apart. I love you, and My love will heal any and every hurt. Embrace My love and live in happiness.

SCRIPTURES

Exodus 15:26; Psalm 147:3; Proverbs 3:5

HEALING PRAYER

Your love for me is unconditional. Help me to walk in healing and forgiveness. Teach me how to love beyond what I may be feeling physically or emotionally. Father, teach me what love looks like as I seek Your face. You are what love looks like. In Jesus' name, amen.

HEALING CONFESSIONS AND COMMANDS ACTIVATION

I CONFESS AND COMMAND that that every wound on my body is healed by the love of God.

I CONFESS AND COMMAND that every emotional wound and trauma is erased and healed now, in Jesus' name.

I CONFESS AND COMMAND that every spiritual incision by the Holy Spirit will bring alignment, correction, healing, and reconstruction to every break, fracture, cut, bruise, injury, sprain, and damage, in Jesus' name.

I CONFESS AND COMMAND that forgiveness will heal my soul and release me from any past and present obligation.

I CONFESS AND COMMAND that no disorder or mental issue will be my portion.

I CONFESS that the love of God is in my heart and I will never walk in unforgiveness, bitterness, resentment, hatred, sadness, depression, oppression, stress, and anxiety, in Jesus' name.

I CONFESS AND COMMAND that my blood pressure is 120 over 70. The life of God flows in my blood and cleanses my arteries of all matter that does not pertain to life, in the name of Jesus Christ (Mark 11:23).

I CONFESS AND COMMAND that autism and any mental disorder is healed, in Jesus' name.

PROVERBS 3:7-8 (NIV)

Do not be wise in your own eyes; fear the Lord and shun evil. This will bring health to your body and nourishment to your bones.

God Nourishes and Heals the Weak

Humble yourself under My mighty hand and I will exalt you in due season. Continue to learn and grow, My child. Do not allow self-pride or people's wisdom to cause you to miss what I have designed for you to walk out before the foundation of the world. Shun away from walking in self-righteousness; walk in humility. Evil traps are set up to snare you.

Avoid ungodly activities that will bring about judgment. I will make a way of escape when the enemy's attempts are overbearing. You will live in peace and good health as you keep My commandments. I will nourish your mind, body, and strengthen you in your old age. Trust that I will heal you and care for you when you need me the most. I will monitor you around the clock; and when you call upon My name, I will come to your bedside.

SCRIPTURES

Isaiah 46:4; 1 Corinthians 10:13; 1 Peter 5:6-7

HEALING PRAYER

Father, You are my daily bread. Your truth liberates me and matures me. When I am weak, send the meat of Your word that will give me the necessary principles to live by. Provide me fresh manna and revelation daily as I seek Your face. In Jesus' name, amen.

HEALING CONFESSIONS AND COMMANDS ACTIVATION

I CONFESS AND COMMAND that when I am weak in my spirit that God makes me stronger in His Spirit.

I CONFESS that the Holy Spirit comes with the necessary boost of energy that infuses my spirit and heart.

I CONFESS AND COMMAND that I release from my heart any harbored unforgiveness, resentment, anger, strife, malice, and hatred toward anyone in authority, my parents, and those who I am to love.

I CONFESS AND COMMAND my heart is healed from the residue of the past, and I am walking in truth and freedom by the Holy Spirit.

I CONFESS that whom the Son of God sets free, they are free indeed.

I CONFESS AND COMMAND that my mind is focused and that I am coherent in speech and memory.

I CONFESS AND COMMAND that my heartbeat is normal. My heart beats with the rhythm of life, carrying the life of God throughout my body, restoring life and health abundantly now (John 17:23; Ephesians 2:22).

PROVERBS 4:20-22 (NLT)

My child, pay attention to what I say. Listen carefully to my words.
Don't lose sight of them. Let them penetrate deep into your heart, for
they bring life to those who find them, and healing to their whole body.

God's Healing Word Will Find You

Incline your ears to My voice today. I have special things I want to share that will help you. My word will become your daily multivitamin and minerals required to maintain a healthy immune system, bones, blood, and life. Do not lose sight of the healing promises in My Word. I come to restore you to wholeness. You will not breakdown nor allow the enemy to take advantage of you. Keep My word close to your heart.

My child, haven't I declared in My Word that faith comes by hearing and hearing by the word of God? Allow My healing power and Word to find you today. It will awaken you and reassure you that everything is well with you and your faith will make you whole. Your faith needs an assignment. My Word has the creative ability to not only bring healing but also saturate you with the healing power to cause you to arise from the ashes of life. You are not a victim of your condition—you are victorious over it.

SCRIPTURES

Proverbs 2:2; Romans 10:17; 1 Corinthians 15:57

HEALING PRAYER

Father God, You have sent Your word to heal me and set me free from those in the past who have tripped me up. I have fallen, but Your hands have come to place me back on my feet. Impart Your wisdom in my heart that I may apply it daily in my walk with Jesus. In Jesus' name, amen.

HEALING CONFESSIONS AND COMMANDS ACTIVATION

I CONFESS that God's healing word spoken over my life will manifest to bring Him glory.

I CONFESS AND COMMAND that I will pay attention to the words of God and keep them close to my heart.

I CONFESS AND COMMAND my blood cells to destroy every disease, germ, bacteria, and virus that try to inhabit my body. I command every cell in my body to be normal, in Jesus' name (Romans 5:17; Luke 17:6).

I CONFESS AND COMMAND that every cell that does not promote life and health in my body is cut off from its source. My immune system will not allow tumorous, cancerous growth to live in my blood cells or body, in Jesus' name (Luke 17:6).

I CONFESS AND COMMAND that my body is sickness- and disease-free, and I command every foreign virus, growth, and disease in my blood cells, streams, and body to leave now, in Jesus' name.

I CONFESS AND COMMAND that my body is sacred and the holy temple of the Holy Spirit.

PROVERBS 17:22 (NIV)

A cheerful heart is good medicine, but a crushed spirit dries up the bones.

God Heals a Cheerful Heart

Ilove to see you happy. Make today count and forget what was done or what was said yesterday. Today brings you new challenges but also excitement. Life at times can be a melting pot of issues and problems. But you don't have to eat what it brews. You have the authority and power by the Holy Spirit to season your life with My wisdom. Times do get hard, but be of good cheer and keep a positive outlook no matter what. A cheerful mentality and heart is a good antidote and medicine for the soul.

Do not allow complaining, murmuring, and resentment to crush you to pieces and cause you to live in a place of no return. I will heal every crushed or broken heart. I will soothe those inner wounds that come to remind you constantly that you have no way to overcome it. Together we will conquer them and your fears. Laugh and live again. Laughter is good for you. I want to make you smile. In My presence, you will receive the peace you are well deserving of and need.

SCRIPTURES

Proverbs 17:22; Philippians 2:14-15; James 1:5-8

HEALING PRAYER

Father, I trust Your decision over my life and what You have destined for me to accomplish. I am not perfect, as You already know, so help me to be the best me that I can be. I don't want to walk in misery but in mercy and happiness. In Jesus' name, amen.

HEALING CONFESSIONS AND COMMANDS ACTIVATION

I CONFESS AND COMMAND that I have a cheerful heart and God is healing me from any pain or hurt.

I CONFESS that the Spirit of God comes to quicken and make alive my mortal body.

I CONFESS and declare that pain, sickness, and hurt will not get the best of me; I overcome them with the Word of God.

I CONFESS AND COMMAND that I am redeemed from the curse of the law and my heart beat flows synchronized to the rhythm of life. The Spirit of life of God's Word flows in me, cleansing my blood of any impurity and every disease (Proverbs 4:20-21).

I CONFESS AND COMMAND that my arteries will not shrink or become clogged up. I command my arteries to function as God has ordained them to and that they are clean, elastic, and not oversized, in Jesus' name (Isaiah 55:11; Mark 11:23; Luke 17:6; James 3:2-5).

I CONFESS AND COMMAND that my mind is focused and that I am coherent in speech and memory.

I CONFESS AND COMMAND that my heartbeat is normal. My heart beats with the rhythm of life, carrying the life of God throughout my body, restoring life and health abundantly now (John 17:23; Ephesians 2:22).

Isaiah 40:31 (NIV)
*But those who hope in the Lord will renew their strength.
They will soar on wings like eagles; they will run and
not grow weary, they will walk and not be faint.*

God Sends a Word for the Weary

Opposition comes to test what you are made of. Seize the moment and recognize that you are being tried and tested to come forth with the answers. Put your confidence in Me, knowing that I know all the answers to life's problems. I know your beginning and your ending. Over time, My child, you will get weary in doing what you are passionate about. I understand that there are times you need to be left alone to iron out the wrinkles that come with responsibilities.

Rely on Me for every solution to every situation and circumstances that emerges. I am your hope, and in Me you will find renewed strength. As you run your personal race to destiny, do not get short of breath in the process, allow Me to send the momentum you need to get you across the finish line. When you faint, I will be your water intake that will replenish what was lost. Healing will be your portion today.

SCRIPTURES

Psalm 118:8, 146:3; Isaiah 40:31

HEALING PRAYER

You send Your Word for those who are weary. I will trust in You with all my heart and lean not to my own understanding but in all my ways acknowledge You so that You will give me direction. My hope is in You only, not in man. Help me to see the finish line of my destiny. In Jesus' name, amen.

HEALING CONFESSIONS AND COMMANDS ACTIVATION

I CONFESS in my heart that God loves me and sends His Word to revive me in my lifeless state.

I CONFESS AND COMMAND that I am walking in total restoration and that deliverance is the children's bread.

I CONFESS that when I am weary God sends His Word of hope to free, encourage, strengthen, edify, build up, and heal me.

I CONFESS that I am walking in the healing, miracle promises of God over my life, and they are not hindered or frustrated.

I CONFESS AND COMMAND that I am no longer disabled, paralyzed, or crippled by what others have said or done or what I have done to myself.

I CONFESS AND COMMAND that my mind is focused and that I am coherent in speech and memory.

I CONFESS AND COMMAND that my blood is working according to how the Lord has ordained it to function and work throughout my body, carrying the life of God throughout my body, restoring life and health abundantly now, in Jesus' name.

ISAIAH 41:10 (NIV)

*So do not fear, for I am with you; do not be dismayed, for
I am your God. I will strengthen you and help you; I
will uphold you with my righteous right hand.*

God Encourages the Discouraged

I have some good news for you, My child. I know that you may have heard something that has brought discouragement or some bad news. But I want you to know that bad news will not dictate the outcome of what I have pre-ordained and predestined for you. Know that I am your Father and I will shake the earth and move the heavens on your behalf so you know that I am serious about your purpose and destiny. I am serious about your health and well-being.

It is My desire to see you fully functioning as I have created and designed you originally to function. I am here to help you. You cannot do everything in your own power. Move your ego or pride aside so that I can bless, heal, and restore you. I will uphold you when you have fallen short of your goals and objectives. You are not perfect, but I will perfect those things concerning you. Hear Me and be healed in your heart.

SCRIPTURES

Psalm 138:8; Romans 8:29; Ephesians 1:5

HEALING PRAYER

I am blessed and fortunate to have a loving and caring Father who will not let me sit in self-pity. Your fatherly counsel and love reassures me that I am not alone. You encourage me when I am discouraged. Heal me from people, places, and things that are not healthy for me. In Jesus' name, amen.

HEALING CONFESSIONS AND COMMANDS ACTIVATION

I CONFESS AND COMMAND that I am no longer what others label me, but what God called me—which is His child.

I CONFESS AND COMMAND that I will no longer think that I am sick, regardless what my body says. The blood of the Lamb heals me.

I CONFESS AND COMMAND that I am encouraged daily by the nutrients of God's Word.

I CONFESS AND COMMAND that I will not allow people to overwhelm me and stress me out.

I CONFESS that in Jesus' name I will not be deceived in any manner. I command my body to not be deceived by any virus or disease, bacteria or germ. Neither will my body work against life or total health in any way. I say that every cell of my body supports life and health (Matthew 12:25,35).

I CONFESS AND COMMAND that mental, physical, and spiritual strength is renewed and restored by faith in God's Word.

I CONFESS AND COMMAND that my immune system is growing stronger day by day. I speak life to my immune system. I forbid confusion in my immune system. The same Spirit who raised Christ from the dead dwells in me and quickens my immune system with the life and wisdom of God, which guards the life and health of my body.

ISAIAH 53:5 (NIV)

But he was pierced for our transgressions; he was crushed
for our iniquities; the punishment that brought us peace
was upon him, and by his wounds we are healed.

God's Word Heals All

Know, My special one, that I sent My Son Jesus into the world to save the world because My love toward it knows no boundaries. His assignment was not only to redeem humanity into right fellowship with Me, but also to heal, deliver, set free, cast out demon spirits, cure disease, and bring wholeness. He was bruised and died for you. Jesus can relate to every situation that you may be facing or have found yourself in.

I understood what you are encountering each day, so I have sent My Word for you to hold, hear, receive, believe, and by faith dismantle every lie of sickness, infirmity, and even sin. My Word is not a Band-Aid to your wounds, it will do spiritual surgery to bring about total recovery. I refuse to allow the enemy to plague your mind and body with drugs, alcohol, and other substances. Your body and mind belong to Me. Turn everything over to Me and I will cleanse you, heal you, deliver you, and restore you from the inside out.

SCRIPTURES

Ezekiel 36:25; John 3:17; 1 John 1:9

HEALING PRAYER

You sent Your only begotten Son Jesus to save the world and relieve us from sickness and any deadly disease. He understands my pain and was crushed for my iniquities. I was once a filthy rag, but now Your word washes me and makes me just in Your sight. In Jesus' name, amen.

HEALING CONFESSIONS AND COMMANDS ACTIVATION

I CONFESS that God's love and Word bring physical and spiritual healing.

I CONFESS AND COMMAND that I have nothing missing, broken, or lacking in my life.

I CONFESS AND COMMAND that laughter brings healing to the soul, and I will continue to laugh daily.

I CONFESS AND COMMAND that my bones are healthy and stronger by the calcium of God's Word.

I CONFESS that the Holy Spirit breathes life over me and burns up any impurity in me.

I CONFESS AND COMMAND that my mind is healthy and my thoughts are acute.

I CONFESS AND COMMAND that my joints will function properly and align to the Word of God. I make demands on my joints to operate as they were designed to function. There is no pain or swelling in my joints, and I command that every ligament, bone, marrow, tissue, muscle, and blood cell will function at 100 percent, in Jesus' name.

I SPEAK to the bones and joints of my body and **I COMMAND** you to be normal, in Jesus' name. I command my bones and joints not to respond to any disease; for the spirit of life of First Peter 2:24 permeates every joint, bone, tissue, muscle, and cell of my body with life and health.

ISAIAH 54:17 (NIV)

"No weapon forged against you will prevail, and you will refute every tongue that accuses you. This is the heritage of the servants of the Lord, and this is their vindication from me," declares the Lord.

God Vindicates His People

There are daily weapons of warfare that are targeted against you. Even though they may be constructed for your demise, they will be disarmed by My Spirit and Power. I will not allow you to be a target or on the devil's hit list. The adversary has a plan and plot to take you out suddenly. Nevertheless, his plans will fall to nothing and will be disabled. Know, My child, that you have been marked for greatness. Sickness, disease, debt, hurt, pain, and sin can cripple you and desensitize your forward progress.

Dislodge yourself from any illegal associations and allegiance that are not for the purpose of the Kingdom. The arsenal attacks planned against you will not prosper nor prevail. There will be slandering tongues and word curses sent to stop you, but they will not harm you in any way. I shall vindicate your name and see to it that you are blessed. I will be your shield of protection from any hurt, harm, and danger. No disease or sickness will take root as you yield to the Holy Spirit's directives daily.

SCRIPTURES

Proverbs 8:33; Isaiah 60; Acts 17:11; 2 Corinthians 1:20

HEALING PRAYER

Father, I thank You for clearing up my name when the enemy comes to throw dirt on it. You use the dirt as fertilizer to grow me into something beautiful and powerful. Cover me with Your wings and hide Me in Your safety place. In Jesus' name, amen.

HEALING CONFESSIONS AND COMMANDS ACTIVATION

I CONFESS AND COMMAND that my good name is being recognized by the Lord and by those who I relate with daily.

I CONFESS AND COMMAND that gossip, slander, and division is not within in my borders and sphere of activities.

I CONFESS that God loves me so much that He gave His only begotten Son for me. I believe in Jesus; therefore, I will not perish. I have eternal life (John 3:16).

I CONFESS AND COMMAND that I am highly favored of the Lord and He esteems me in everything that I do in Him.

I CONFESS that Christ, the Anointed One and His anointing, is in me through the Holy Spirit. He is my peace, joy, hope, and expectation of glory (Colossians 1:27).

I CONFESS AND COMMAND that financial debt from medical bills will not overtake me; the Father will give me a settlement plan to pay back what I owe and supernatural blessings to get out of debt.

I CONFESS AND COMMAND that I am not conformed to this world. I am transformed as I renew my mind to God's Word. I experience the good, acceptable, and perfect will of God (Romans 12:2).

ISAIAH 57:19 (NIV)

"Creating praise on their lips. Peace, peace, to those far and near," says the Lord. "And I will heal them."

God Heals Through Praise

Life has the potential to place unnecessary burdens and demands on you. Having to juggle them all and also bring balance to your life can be overwhelming. The enemy comes like a python to immobilize you from progressing. Its grip is purposed to crush you as you inhale and take a breather. You are crushed and broken into pieces. I get it, My child, you need a place to vent. In My presence is where you can be yourself and share everything on your heart, and you will not be judged. Let your hair down and relax in My presence. There is no condemnation unto those who are in Christ Jesus, My Son.

You can breathe easy and put a praise on your lips. Your praise will become like sweet aroma from a rose to My nostrils. Your praise will scatter your enemy and give them a black eye. Through your praise, you release Heaven to respond on your behalf. Through your praise and song of praise, you are brought out of the darkest moments and allowed to see the light. Your praise is the ingredient that will heal you and bring joy into your life. Do not settle in that mud-like condition; rather, spring forth into living, healing waters.

SCRIPTURES

Romans 8:1; Hebrews 13:15

HEALING PRAYER

My praise will be a weapon of warfare against the enemy. The adversary does not want me made whole and walking in complete assurance of who I am in Christ. I am speaking divine healing over every area of my life and family. My praise will be the vehicle to divine healing and breakthrough. In Jesus' name, amen.

HEALING CONFESSIONS AND COMMANDS ACTIVATION

I CONFESS AND COMMAND that through my praise I will have personal victory.

I CONFESS AND COMMAND that my praise will scatter the plans of the enemy and the Father will send warring angels on my behalf to war.

I CONFESS AND COMMAND that I can do all things through Christ—the Anointed One—and His power will heal and strengthen me (Philippians 4:13).

I CONFESS AND COMMAND that I am highly favored of the Lord and He esteems me in everything that I do in Him.

I CONFESS AND COMMAND that I do not allow the worries of this world or the deceitfulness of riches or the lusts of other things to enter into my heart, mind, or soul to choke out the Word of God. I am determined to produce much fruit (Mark 4:19).

I CONFESS AND COMMAND that my praise is a weapon against the enemy.

I CONFESS AND COMMAND that I will not walk in pain or agony, but in healing and freedom.

ISAIAH 58:8 (NIV)

Then your light will break forth like the dawn, and your healing will quickly appear; then your righteousness will go before you, and the glory of the Lord will be your rear guard.

God's Healing Light

Feel the warmth of My presence when you commune with Me today. I will shine new insight and revelation into your life. The systems of this world can be cruel and coldhearted at times. Do not allow this to shake you or alter your decision to seek My face daily for answers to your questions. If you feel like you are in your night season, just look around and wait for the dawn of My glory light that will break forth.

Healing will come to you and everything that needs My touch. Healing will be your inheritance by faith because you anticipated it. Reach up and grab hold of what you have been seeking and asking Me for. Know that I desire to see you well and blooming like the lily in the valley. When you are parched, I will soak your thirst; and when you are dry and brittle, I will saturate you with My refreshing Spirit. I will honor you with love and satisfy your years with pleasure. Rest in Me and know that I will be your healing agent.

SCRIPTURES

Deuteronomy 4:29; Psalm 62:5-12; 91:16

HEALING PRAYER

Daddy-God, I want to feel Your healing presence today. Shine Your divine glory light on me that I will revive and awaken from stagnation. I want to see clearly in this season and break free from any limitation and invisible walls around me. In Jesus' name, amen.

HEALING CONFESSIONS AND
COMMANDS ACTIVATION

I CONFESS AND COMMAND that the healing light of Christ will shine on every dark place in my life and bring healing power and heat to those areas in my body.

I CONFESS AND COMMAND that I will hearken unto the Word of God concerning personal healing and deliverance. All the blessings of the Word of God will come on me and overtake me (Deuteronomy 28:2).

I CONFESS AND COMMAND that I am a believer, and all things are possible to me because I believe (Mark 9:23).

I CONFESS AND COMMAND that I will never walk in ignorance; revelation knowledge will be my portion.

I CONFESS that the Holy Spirit will come to my aid and bear me up in my weakness when I do not know how to pray as I ought for healing or deliverance. He intercedes on my behalf according to the will of God (Romans 8:26-27).

I CONFESS AND COMMAND that all God's healing promises that Jesus bore for me are already done at the cross.

I CONFESS that the Lord is my rear guard and His glory light shines brighter each day.

ISAIAH 61:1-3 (NIV)

The Spirit of the Sovereign Lord is on me, because the Lord has anointed me to preach good news to the poor. He has sent me to bind up the brokenhearted, to proclaim freedom for the captives and release from darkness for the prisoners, to proclaim the year of the Lord's favor and the day of vengeance of our God, to comfort all who mourn, and provide for those who grieve in Zion—to bestow on them a crown of beauty instead of ashes, the oil of gladness instead of mourning, and a garment of praise instead of a spirit of despair....

God Will Mantle You with Healing Powers

I have created you so a river of healing will flow out of you. You contain the power to bring things into being by the very words you speak. Life and death is in the power of your tongue. Utilize that instrument that is vital in your mouth. It is time to discover your spiritual potential and maximize it for My glory. Never second-guess yourself and what I have given you before you were born.

Tap into your reserved potential and release the power of the Holy Spirit. You were created for so much more. Do not live beneath your means; live beyond your needs that are hidden in Me and watch Me supply your needs. I will anoint you with the Holy Spirit's enablement, and you will be a healing vessel that will bring change and lasting result to your generation. Together as a divine partnership, we can accomplish great things.

SCRIPTURES
Psalm 18:21; Philippians 4:19

HEALING PRAYER

Father, You have made me unique and I am special in Your sight. Give me the grace to fulfill the purposes of the Kingdom here and now. Fill up my cup, Lord, that it will run over and bless those who are hungry and thirsty. In Jesus' name, amen.

HEALING CONFESSIONS AND COMMANDS ACTIVATION

I CONFESS AND COMMAND that the mantle of healing rest upon me, and I am stronger today than yesterday.

I CONFESS that the Spirit of God is upon me, for He has anointed me with power.

I CONFESS that God has given me a beauty for ashes and the oil of gladness instead of mourning. I am cloaked with the garment of praise instead of the spirit of despair.

I CONFESS AND COMMAND that the blessing of Abraham comes on me through Jesus Christ. I receive the promise of the Spirit through faith. I am an heir to the promise of God (Galatians 3:14,29).

I CONFESS AND COMMAND that I have divine access to the healing power of God through the Holy Spirit. I can lay hands on myself and release the healing virtue of Christ.

I CONFESS AND COMMAND that I have access by faith into the grace of God (Romans 5:2).

I CONFESS AND COMMAND that I repent and turn daily away from sin or anything that will cause sickness or disease, in Jesus' name.

I CONFESS that the Kingdom of God is here and now in my life (Matthew 4:17).

JEREMIAH 17:14 (NIV)

Heal me, Lord, and I will be healed; save me and I will be saved, for you are the one I praise.

God Heals and Saves Those Who Ask

If you ask Me to heal you, why would you doubt that I cannot? I can do the impossible. If you ask Me to deliver or save you, why would My arms be too short to help you? When you call upon My name to heal those broken areas of your life, I will come like a Master Potter, put you on the potter's wheel, and smooth out the rough places while plugging up the holes that are there. I will refine you and make you anew again.

I will shape you into that self-same image of My Son Jesus when I am done processing you. I hear you every time you speak. My ears are attentive to your voice. You have a special ring tone that is designated just for you. You are not a number in a factory inventory list; you are My prized possession, and I am here to deliver you and heal you and set you on the right path of divine rehabilitation.

SCRIPTURES

Psalm 91:15; Jeremiah 33:3; Romans 8:29

HEALING PRAYER

When my voice is weak, You still hear and respond. Father, there are times when my expectations are high and demands are too, help me to keep my end of the agreement. As I learn to continue walking in obedience to Your will for my life, I pray that that nothing is missing, broken or lacking. In Jesus' name, amen.

HEALING CONFESSIONS AND
COMMANDS ACTIVATION

I CONFESS AND COMMAND that God will heal every place that needs healing and bring salvation to those I ask Him to touch in a special way.

I CONFESS AND COMMAND that my hope is anchored in the Lord Jesus Christ and His hope keeps me sure and steadfast (Hebrews 6:19).

I CONFESS AND COMMAND that healing is in my mouth and I can declare the wonderful works of Christ and receive what He has already defeated 2,000 years ago for me.

I CONFESS AND COMMAND that my prayers and supplications for healing are met, and I am not *going* to be healed—I *am* healed.

I CONFESS AND COMMAND that I reverently fear the Lord daily and I respect, honor, and bless Him; therefore, I do not lack anything (Psalm 34:9).

I CONFESS AND COMMAND that in God's presence there is healing forevermore.

I CONFESS AND COMMAND that my life is not short-circuited by any sin or unresolved issues. I release them unto the Lord and detox my mind, body, and soul with the Word of the Lord.

JEREMIAH 29:11 (NIV)

"For I know the plans I have for you," declares the Lord, "plans to prosper you and not to harm you, plans to give you hope and a future."

God has a Plan to Prosper You

Good morning, My loved one. I have watched over you, waiting in excitement for you to awaken. As your eyes opened, it brought a big smile on My face. I waited in anticipation to see you seek My face and allow Me to bring clear direction, guidance, and insight into your day. I know your body, mind, and spirit may be a little beat up and you feel restless or even fatigue. Allow My Spirit to heal and rejuvenate you in spite of what you are going through.

Keep the faith and know that My thoughts toward you are not of evil but a bright and promising future. Believe what I am sharing with you today. Confess that you are healed today and meditate on it daily. Release your faith for not only personal healing, but for a miracle breakthrough that you see coming to you. There are people waiting for you to get better to help them get better. This condition is not unto death! You are a fighter and survivor. I am rooting you on. Sickness and diseases will not stop you. Why? Because Jesus settled it once and for all on the cross 2,000 years ago. He put an end to hopelessness so that you will have a future.

SCRIPTURES

Jeremiah 29:11; 1 Timothy 6:12

HEALING PRAYER

Father, You have my best interest at heart. You provide all of my needs when I seek You for clear direction. I realize that even an evil person knows how to give good gifts to those they love. You are a loving Father, teach me how to model Christ in everything I do and say. In Jesus' name, amen.

HEALING CONFESSIONS AND COMMANDS ACTIVATION

I CONFESS that God will prosper the works of my hands in obedience to the His Word.

I CONFESS and declare that God has bestowed His grace upon me, and by His grace I am what I am (1 Corinthians 15:10).

I CONFESS that I am a child of God and healing is the will of God for my life.

I CONFESS AND COMMAND that I am free from any ungodly obligation, agreement, oaths, and promises that are not sent by the Lord.

I CONFESS AND COMMAND that all authority in Heaven and on earth has been given to me by Jesus Christ, and I crush sickness and disease that try to enter into my life illegally (Matthew 28:18).

I CONFESS AND COMMAND that the doctor's report may say one thing, but my second and only opinion is the will of God; and His will is to see me healed, set free, and blessed.

I CONFESS AND COMMAND that I forgive those whom I have anything against so that my prayers are not hindered. I will make it my business to reach out to every one of them to apologize and to release myself (Mark 11:25).

JUDE 24-25 (NIV)

To him who is able to keep you from stumbling and to present you before his glorious presence without fault and with great joy—to the only God our Savior be glory, majesty, power and authority, through Jesus Christ our Lord, before all ages, now and forevermore! Amen.

God Will not let you Fall

Arise and take up your bed and walk, My child. Get motivated about your future. I know what the enemy has declared over you. I come that you might have life and have it more abundantly. Know, My child, that I will provide you with the daily supplement that is required to take in by faith to run this race with endurance. At times, you do not have enough strength to muster up, but I am with you and by your side.

I will not just sit here and watch the enemy kick you while you are down. I will send My angels to keep you from falling and place you back on the right path of purpose. Let us implement a plan of recovery that works best for you. Have I not said in My Word that faith without works is dead? I want to work your faith and build the spiritual muscles that will give the devil a knockout. You are not what the doctor says or what your conditions says. I have the last word and final answer to your solution, problem, issue, circumstance, sickness, and disease. I declare over you that you shall recover quickly and recover all that has been taken from you.

SCRIPTURES
James 1:14-26; Mark 2:9; John 5:8

HEALING PRAYER

When I took my first step as a child, Father, You were there. Likewise, when I took my first spiritual step as a babe in Christ, You were there. Identify any detours and traps set before me by the enemy. Give me deer feet to jump over them, and give me sight as an eagle to see them up ahead. In Jesus' name, amen.

HEALING CONFESSIONS AND COMMANDS ACTIVATION

I CONFESS AND COMMAND that I will not fall into sin and God will keep me from stumbling.

I CONFESS that I will stand on the promises of the Lord over my life, which serves as a sure foundation for living a godly lifestyle in Christ.

I CONFESS AND COMMAND that I will continue to resist the devil by the authority of Christ in me and he will flee.

I CONFESS that God has given me every place that my feet tread upon. Therefore, I have dominion and authority over sin, sickness, and poverty, in Jesus' name (Joshua 1:3).

I CONFESS AND COMMAND that I am the head and not the tail, first and not last, above and not beneath.

I CONFESS AND COMMAND this is my time of coming out with victory and power in Christ.

I CONFESS AND COMMAND that the Spirit of the Lord is upon me and He has anointed me with the same anointing that Jesus possessed when He was here on the earth. This anointing in me removes all fears, doubt, burdens, and destroys every yoke in my life, in Jesus' name (Luke 4:18; Isaiah 10:27).

JEREMIAH 30:17

"But I will restore you to health and heal your wounds," declares the Lord, "because you are called an outcast, Zion for whom no one cares."

God Brings Divine Health and Restoration

Believe the words that I declare over you. These are not mere words. My Words are Spirit and life. I am releasing a supernatural miracle in your life that will shock those whoever doubted. In My presence there is tranquility and peace. In this place you will receive the rest that your body and spirit is thirsty for. Pray in the Spirit and fill yourself up on your most holy faith. Give me something to work with as you speak your healing and restoration by faith.

Co-create with Me in your own circumstances. Things are the way they are because maybe you are the way you are. You are what I made you to be. Align your thoughts toward what My Word says you are. Think on those things that are above and not beneath you. In other words, My beloved, think on things that are spiritual and not carnal or earthly. I want to heal you in every way—soul, mind, and body. Change your perspective about healing and miracles. They are not things of the past, nor is deliverance. I am God enough to create the universe, and I am also God enough to release a creative miracle for you if you ask Me. Think on healing, speak on healing, hear the words of healing—and *be healed* today!

SCRIPTURES

John 6:63; Colossians 3:2

HEALING PRAYER

I may be an outcast or strange to the world. But Daddy-God, You have fearfully and wonderfully created me like You. Bring restoration in my life that will cause me to live the life You so desire for me to live. It's a spiritual life that requires sacrifice, love, and continual commitment to You only. Show me how to receive my breakthrough and miracle now. In Jesus' name, amen.

HEALING CONFESSIONS AND COMMANDS ACTIVATION

I CONFESS that God will bring divine health and restoration to every area of my life and body now, in Jesus' name.

I CONFESS that God has dealt to me the measure of faith, and this type of faith is the God type and nature of faith to believe for the impossible for my life (Romans 12:3).

I CONFESS that God sees the best in me and not the worse and that my outcome in life will always be positive.

I CONFESS AND COMMAND that I expect daily the glory of God to be poured out on my life like rain when I am in the presence of God seeking His face and touch (Zechariah 10:1).

I CONFESS AND COMMAND that I refuse to be deceived or misled by having evil associations, networks, alliances, and companions that are unhealthy to my spiritual growth. I choose to fellowship and collaborate with those who believe in the Lord Jesus Christ (1 Corinthians 15:33).

I CONFESS AND COMMAND that healing and deliverance is not outdated but something for the present and future and those in need of God's healing power.

JEREMIAH 33:6 (NIV)
Nevertheless, I will bring health and healing to it; I will heal my people and will let them enjoy abundant peace and security.

God Brings Peace, Security, and Healing

Awake and eat, My child. I have living bread that is coming down from Heaven for you to consume. This bread is the children's bread that has been reserved especially for you. It contains the healing and nourishment needed for your whole health. I want to deliver you and cause you to enjoy life. There are things that will come to rob you of your peace, joy, and righteousness. I sent My Son Jesus to restore that which was lost and hopeless.

I will bring health and release supernatural healing for which you stand in dire need. Be sober and vigilant and understand, My child, that the devil is as a roaring lion seeking to devour those who belong to Me. When he attacks you to try to kill you, know that I will come to your aid and snatch you from his hungry bite. I will heal and protect you so that you can live in harmony in My presence.

SCRIPTURES

John 6:51; 1 Peter 5:8; 1 Thessalonians 5:23-28

HEALING PRAYER

Father, loose me from any evil devices that come to set me up to fail and fall. Heal my heart from things that are not relevant now and keep me pondering on things of the past. Sin will cause sickness and unforgiveness will become like cancer to the bones. Detox me, Father, so I am free and whole. In Jesus' name, amen.

HEALING CONFESSIONS AND COMMANDS ACTIVATION

I CONFESS that the peace *of* God is with me and peace *with* God is upon me daily.

I CONFESS that I am safe in the presence of God, and there I find refuge.

I CONFESS that when I am not myself, in God's presence there is love and peace that surpass all my understanding.

I CONFESS AND COMMAND that none of my expectations are my own but God's expectation for greatness to come forth from my life.

I CONFESS AND COMMAND that every unhealthy relationship is removed and God is sending people into my life with pure hearts and clean hands to work for Kingdom advancement.

I CONFESS AND COMMAND that the weak shall say they are strong; and I decree that in my weakness I am mighty in the Holy Spirit.

I CONFESS that Jesus' blood came to destroy the powers of death, hell, and the grave. His delivering power has destroyed every work of the devil in my life, and He has delivered me from the bondage of fear, in Jesus' name (Romans 12:1).

MALACHI 4:2

But to you who fear My name the sun of righteousness shall arise with healing in His wings; and you shall go out grow fat like stall-fed calves.

God's Healing Wings

Good morning, My child. I have been thinking about you. What concerns you, concerns Me as well. I know it is a fight thinking about your condition and health each day and trying to make sense of it all. Did you know that My Son Jesus was bruised for your guilt and iniquities, and that the chastisement needed to obtain your peace and well-being was upon Him? He endured the lashes and beating so that you may live and soar in your personal healing.

He will come with healing in His wings and deliver you from oppression, depression, stress, pain, agony, hurt, ridicule, persecution, and heart-wrenching thoughts. Your affiliation will not endure any longer. I call forth divine healing now for you, My child, so that you are perfectly made whole. There is no sickness or disease in Heaven, and I desire that on earth you do not experience it either. Then we will meet face to face at the appointed time. Ride the wings of healing by faith and watch Me send the fire of revival to where you are.

SCRIPTURES

Exodus 14:14; Isaiah 53:5; Malachi 4:2

HEALING PRAYER

Rescue me from the sins that try to tempt me today, Father. Give me a sanctified imagination to filter out what is You and what is the influence of the evil one. I am not alone; You guide my feet on the right path. Swoop me up like an eagle would do with her eaglet and deliver me from the predators of my destiny. In Jesus' name, amen.

HEALING CONFESSIONS AND COMMANDS ACTIVATION

I CONFESS that my healing is in God's healing wings.

I CONFESS AND COMMAND that what I am looking for is looking for me and what I am praying for has been sent exponentially to me.

I CONFESS that I present my body to God daily as a living sacrifice. I will live a holy life, which is acceptable unto Him, that is my reasonable worship unto Him (Romans 12:1).

I CONFESS AND COMMAND that I will stay constantly in prayer, believing what I have received of God by faith and walk in it.

I CONFESS AND COMMAND that death and life are in the power of my tongue and I am determined daily to speak words of life, healing, restoration, power, miracles, and blessings (Proverbs 18:21).

I CONFESS that I would suffer in the flesh daily rather than fail to please my God daily (1 Peter 4:1).

MATTHEW 4:23-25 (NIV)

*Jesus went throughout Galilee, teaching in their synagogues,
preaching the good news of the kingdom, and healing every
disease and sickness among the people. News about him spread
all over Syria, and people brought to him all who were ill
with various diseases, those suffering severe pain, the demon-
possessed, those having seizures, and the paralyzed, and he healed
them. Large crowds from Galilee, the Decapolis, Jerusalem,
Judea and the region across the Jordan followed him.*

God's Kingdom of Healing

Wake up today with an expectation to see Me more in an unusual way. I am sending love notes to you this day to express My heart toward you. My unfailing love and unconditional commitment to you will not be broken. You can bring any issue, problem, disease, sickness, suffering, severe pain, affliction, and disabling situation to Me—and watch Me perform a miracle. I am the God of the impossible.

I do not shy away from working miracles and healing those who call upon Me to do this. I love to display My mighty handiwork in your day. Be encouraged and know that I am working things out, whether the issue or concern may look impossible to work on. I am the Surgeon of surgeons, Doctor of doctors, Physician of physicians, and Healer of healers. Regardless how big or small the sickness or circumstance may appear, I can a turn a mountain into a valley and a valley into a mountain. Trust Me, your Father, and have faith that your healing is coming today.

SCRIPTURES

Matthew 8; Luke 18:27

HEALING PRAYER

Shine Your light upon my cloudy mind and allow me to see Your glory in such a way that I will not walk in doubt. I want to learn more about Your supernatural Kingdom. I am your joint-heir with Christ Jesus. In Jesus' name, amen.

HEALING CONFESSIONS AND COMMANDS ACTIVATION

I CONFESS that God's Kingdom is a supernatural Kingdom that releases healings, miracles, and deliverance to those who believe and receive Christ.

I CONFESS AND COMMAND that I am in constant prayer and my prayer times with the Lord will not be hindered or frustrated (Romans 12:12).

I CONFESS AND COMMAND that I do not let my heart be troubled or heartbroken by wicked people, because I trust and abide in Jesus.

I CONFESS that the Lord delivers and saves me out of all my personal afflictions (Psalm 34:19).

I CONFESS and declare that when I touch and agree by faith with another believer about anything that we ask, whether it's for healing, a miracle, blessing, favor, deliverance, or an answer from God, that it shall be done for us by our heavenly Father (Matthew 18:19 NASB).

I CONFESS AND COMMAND that the message of the Kingdom will not depart from my heart and I will study it daily to get understanding.

I CONFESS AND COMMAND that the Kingdom of God is moving in me and through me each day.

MATTHEW 8:5-10 (NIV)

When Jesus had entered Capernaum, a centurion came to him, asking for help. "Lord," he said, "my servant lies at home paralyzed, suffering terribly." Jesus said to him, "Shall I come and heal him?" The centurion replied, "Lord, I do not deserve to have you come under my roof. But just say the word, and my servant will be healed. For I myself am a man under authority, with soldiers under me. I tell this one, 'Go,' and he goes; and that one, 'Come,' and he comes. I say to my servant, 'Do this,' and he does it." When Jesus heard this, he was amazed and said to those following him, "Truly I tell you, I have not found anyone in Israel with such great faith."

God Responds to Faith-Working Miracles

Come up higher, My child, in your faith. I am increasing your capacity to contain more of Me. I will not leave you in a place where you are content with what hand you have been dealt. I know things may not make sense right now, but clarity comes in My word. Stay in My presence and allow Me to change your perspective and outlook on what I can do. I will bring supernatural assistance. I know there are days that are worse off than other days. However, I will come to heal and render My helping hands.

You shall arise up and declare victory over the enemy. Your faith in believing My Word will accelerate the miracle process. I will break natural laws to get my healing power and miracles to you. Have supernatural faith like the centurion who had authority and wanted Jesus to just send the word of miracle to the one who was paralyzed and suffering deeply. My Word will mobilize the paralyzed and bring ease to the disease. I am sending My Word of healing to you. Receive and rise!

SCRIPTURES

Psalm 107:20; Luke 14:10; Revelation 11:12

HEALING PRAYER

Give me great faith like that man who came to Jesus looking for Him to send the word of healing by faith. Increase my faith each day, Father, to trust You for personal revival, transformation, and restoration. I overcome and come through every situation that I face. In Jesus' name, amen.

HEALING CONFESSIONS AND COMMANDS ACTIVATION

I CONFESS that God is responding to my prayers of faith and working miracles daily for me.

I CONFESS AND COMMAND that miracles are my portion and God is always in the healing business.

I CONFESS AND COMMAND that deadly habits of unforgiveness, impatience, rudeness, pride, irritation, and selfishness will loose me and let me go. I choose to walk in total freedom by the power of God's Word (John 11:43-44; Romans 8:2-6).

I CONFESS AND COMMAND that my faith will move every mountain in my path and my faith is not shaken.

I CONFESS that the angels of the Lord have gone before me to make every crooked place straight for me to walk.

I CONFESS AND COMMAND that my faith is rooted and grounded in the Word of God.

MATTHEW 8:14-15 (NIV)

When Jesus came into Peter's house, he saw Peter's mother-in-law lying in bed with a fever. He touched her hand and the fever left her, and she got up and began to wait on him.

God's Healing and Miracle Touch

My beloved one, I have come to check on you. I am here for you. I haven't gone anywhere. I am right by your side. Know, My child, that illness will not keep you stuck for very long. Allow My Word to become a spiritual antibiotic that will kill every demonic bacterium that has plagued you. Whether you feel fatigue in your muscles, joints, and in your body, I will become strength to you. There are times when you may feel too weak to respond in worship, but I examine your heart and faith.

Did you know that faith moves Me and I will heal you with My miracle touch? Allow me to lay My hands on you while you are stabilized. You will feel the heat of My presence. Take a deep breath and let me do inner surgery. It is OK to take time out of the game because everyone needs a break to rest. Know that I am your Life Coach and will help you strategize with a playbook to win the game of life. In My presence, you will receive your goals and objectives to execute. Your healing is here. Just receive the ball given and run toward the touchdown marker. We will win and be victors, defeating all foes.

SCRIPTURES

Isaiah 41:10; Philippians 4:13; 1 Corinthians 15:57

HEALING PRAYER

Touch me, Father, so I will receive Your heavenly impartation. Allow me to live in a realm of possibilities. I repent that my faith has not been at the level it should be. I know that over time it will increase as I see Your miracle touch working in me and through me. In Jesus' name, amen.

HEALING CONFESSIONS AND
COMMANDS ACTIVATION

I CONFESS AND COMMAND that the healing power of God is touching every sensitive place in my life.

I CONFESS AND COMMAND that I will press toward the mark of the high calling in Christ Jesus.

I CONFESS AND COMMAND that as I receive communion, I put myself in remembrance of what Jesus has already done for me through His death on the cross. Knowing that through Jesus I am redeemed from the curse of the law (1 Corinthians 11:25-34; Galatians 3:13).

I CONFESS AND COMMAND that I refuse to permit jealousy, envy, a competition spirit, and strife to take root in my heart. I refuse to give the devil room and license to bring discord, confusion, division, and every evil work into my life (James 3:16).

I CONFESS that Jesus is my Savior and life support when I am on the ventilator of life.

I CONFESS AND COMMAND that I am a living and breathing miracle, and sickness and disease has no place in my life.

MATTHEW 8:16-17 (NIV)

*When evening came, many who were demon-possessed were brought
to him, and he drove out the spirits with a word and healed all
the sick. This was to fulfill what was spoken through the prophet
Isaiah: "He took up our infirmities and bore our diseases."*

God Brings Deliverance and Heals Diseases

Good morning, My loved one. I know your weaknesses and all of your personal struggles. Crave for Me and thirst for Me. Allow Me to be your daily supplement and substance. You do not have to depend or rely on things that will only give you a temporary thrill. In My presence there is joy, peace, and love forevermore. When you are oppressed by evil spirits, I will come as the Terminator and drive them out.

Take back your life. It was given to you to steward. Receive My love that doesn't judge you, see your self-worth and push yourself up. Allow your discontentment of your present state to be a motivating factor and game changer. I will take away the spirit of infirmities that comes like a leech. I will remove every sickness and disease that has come when things are going well. Rise up with victory and use the sword of the Spirit to cut off the excess baggage.

SCRIPTURES

1 Samuel 16:7; Psalm 65:5-12; John 5:22

HEALING PRAYER

Heal my heart so I will receive my portion. I do not want to be like the prodigal son wasting my inheritance; I want to be responsible over what You have entrusted into my care. Father, deliver me from myself and loose the ungodly attachments. In Jesus' name, amen.

HEALING CONFESSIONS AND COMMANDS ACTIVATION

I CONFESS AND COMMAND that evil spirits and the things of my past do not bind me.

I CONFESS AND COMMAND that every negative influence and curse is broken by the Word of God, sword of the Spirit, and by the word of my testimony.

I CONFESS AND COMMAND that deliverance is my daily bread and I will not eat the crumbs from my King's table because I am one of His.

I CONFESS AND COMMAND that my best days are ahead of me and my worse days are behind me.

I CONFESS that I am strong in the Lord and in the power of His might daily (Ephesians 6:10).

I CONFESS AND COMMAND that I will flow in the fruit of the Spirit and permit love, joy, peace, longsuffering, gentleness, goodness, faith, meekness, and temperance to be cultivated in my character and temperament daily (Galatians 5:22-23).

MATTHEW 9:35-36 (NIV)

Jesus went through all the towns and villages, teaching in their synagogues, preaching the good news of the kingdom and healing every disease and sickness. When he saw the crowds, he had compassion on them, because they were harassed and helpless, like sheep without a shepherd.

God's Word Brings Healing to the Hopeless

Open your heart today to what I desire to reveal to you. In My Kingdom, My beloved, there is nothing that can penetrate it or break you. The message of the Kingdom contains life-changing and demon-evicting truth that will revolutionize your thinking. I want to raise the bar of your expectation by helping you reach higher so that you are stretched to do the impossible. The Good News that is heralded is a message that will break personal yokes, liberate those who are bound, raise the dead, and cure all kinds of diseases.

Sin can bring about sicknesses, illnesses, and diseases. However, Jesus has come to relieve you from the curse of sin, death, and the grave. Through the truth of My Word, My child, you will feel your physical and spiritual condition change for the better and not the worse. I am your Hope; you do not have to be hopeless, but hopeful. Your condition will only move me to compassion to act now on your behalf.

SCRIPTURES

Proverbs 4:22; Psalm 62:5; Matthew
14:14; Romans 6:12; 1 John 3:9

HEALING PRAYER

Father, I am grateful for Your Kingdom coming to me in a new way. I am a child of the King. I am healed and set free by the plagues of the world. I am engrafted into Your marvelous Kingdom. Father, help me to shine Your light brighter than before. In Jesus' name, amen.

HEALING CONFESSIONS AND COMMANDS ACTIVATION

I CONFESS that God's Word brings total healing to every need that is present before Him in prayer.

I CONFESS that Jesus is my Hope and the center of my joy.

I CONFESS AND COMMAND that I will live in peace, joy, and righteousness in the Holy Spirit daily.

I CONFESS AND COMMAND that I am obedient to the commandment of Jesus as I study the Word of God and learn to be more like Him in word and deed.

I CONFESS AND COMMAND that I am not down but up; and that I am not the forsaken by Christ but redeemed.

I CONFESS that I will be obedient daily to the voice of God by the Holy Spirit and will love others as He loves me (John 13:34).

MATTHEW 10:7-8 (NIV)

He called his twelve disciples to him and gave them authority to drive out impure spirits and to heal every disease and sickness. As you go, preach this message: "The kingdom of heaven has come near." Heal the sick, raise the dead, cleanse those who have leprosy, drive out demons. Freely you have received; freely give.

God Drives Out Evil Spirits of Affliction

Let Me empower you with the healing virtue and power that has the ability to raise the dead, heal the sick, cure the diseased, give sight to the blind, open deaf ears, cleanse those impure, and deliver those who are oppressed by evil influences. I have sent the Holy Spirit to you to help you and raise you up to be effective in your generation. Arise today, My child, and know that I have sent My Holy Spirit who will teach you all things. The Holy Spirit will equip, teach, counsel, and inspire you to do what you do not do in your own strength.

Depend on Me to show you what you possess within. Embrace the greatness that has been imparted before the foundation of the world. I have given you a tremendous anointing by the Holy Spirit to be the conduit of healing and deliverance. Even though you may be in need of a personal touch from Me, look within yourself and discover the gift of Me in you and unlock your potential to be a world changer. It is I, My child, understand that I have freely given you the gift and freely release it to those in need of the healing, delivering power of the Holy Spirit.

SCRIPTURES
Job 19:21; John 14:16,26

HEALING PRAYER

You deliver me from hurt, harm, and danger. You set my feet on a straight and narrow path that leads to eternal life. Keep my mind stayed on You, that I will not entertain anything that doesn't represent You. In Jesus' name, amen.

HEALING CONFESSIONS AND COMMANDS ACTIVATION

I CONFESS AND COMMAND that there are no illegal spirits invading my space and are evicted by the Holy Spirit, in Jesus' name.

I CONFESS that Jesus endured the cross for me and I am liberated by faith in Christ.

I CONFESS AND COMMAND and declare that there is no condemnation unto those who are in Christ Jesus; I am protected by His blood.

I CONFESS that by the authority of Jesus in me that I can place all things at the feet of Jesus in my life, that are not His will for my life.

I CONFESS that the Kingdom of God is near in my life and I see the delivering power of its presence.

I CONFESS AND COMMAND that health and long life is my portion as I hear daily the Holy Spirit's directions and obey Christ's commandments. I come against the spirit of premature death and accidents waiting to happen, in Jesus' name.

MATTHEW 13:58 (NIV)
And he did not do many miracles there because of their lack of faith.

God Wants to See Your Faith

*B*elieve on My Word and trust every word that you read or hear My Holy Spirit speaking to you as you are in My Presence. Don't allow fear, doubt, and unbelief steal your breakthrough. It is the plan of the enemy to intimidate you and cause you to walk in fear and unbelief, not understanding the truth of My Word. My Son Jesus could only do limited miracles because of the spirit of familiarity and commonality. The spirit of familiarity, My child, will stop up the flow of healing and miracles to be released.

I desire to heal and bring perpetual breakthrough in your life, your family, your city, your community, and your nation. Lack of faith is the enemy of the supernatural power of the Holy Spirit. Load your faith with hearing the words that come from Me. Change your perspective, scope, and worldview, and think on those things above and not earthly. See from My heavenly lenses what I desire to do in your time and generation. You are one I will use to bring about life-altering changes that will affect many for My glory.

SCRIPTURES

2 Samuel 5:20; Romans 10:17; Acts 10:38

HEALING PRAYER

Lord, You know the areas of my heart that need mending and fixing. You don't judge me like people do, You give me a solution and choice to make a change. Increase my faith to believe in Your miracle-working power in my life and to release it for others. In Jesus' name, amen.

HEALING CONFESSIONS AND COMMANDS ACTIVATION

I CONFESS AND COMMAND that I shall walk by faith daily and not by what I see in the natural.

I CONFESS AND COMMAND that I will put my faith to work and in action in my life.

I CONFESS AND COMMAND that I will walk in the wisdom of God and possess a heart of humility.

I CONFESS that Jesus is the High Priest of my profession; therefore, I hold fast to it daily in my life (Hebrews 4:14).

I CONFESS AND COMMAND that I shall give homage, thanks, and praises to the Lord, for He is good to me. His unconditional love and mercy endures forever (Psalm 136:1)

I CONFESS AND COMMAND that I will pursue earnestly and eagerly to love God. I will make it my business and aim to fulfill what the Lord called me to do without any wavering.

I CONFESS AND COMMAND that God is love and He expresses that love in my life as I am in His presence. As I dwell and continue in Him, He lives and continues in me; and love is brought to completion and attains perfection in me (1 John 4:16-17).

MATTHEW 14:36 (NIV)
*And begged him to let the sick just touch the edge of
his cloak, and all who touched it were healed.*

God's Healing Power Activated by Faith

As you draw near to Me, I will draw near to you. I know that you may be feeling not your best at times, but it is those moments that I utilize to display My love and power to you. I can make the unbeliever a believer. I have the ability to touch those most sensitive and vulnerable places of your heart even when you are standing in line for a miracle. I have heard your petition, prayer, and supplication, and I am coming to fulfill your order.

As you say within yourself, *Why me?* or *Why did this have to happen to me?* Don't break down or feel sorry for yourself. Refocus on My Word and My promises as you think on what you want Me to do for you. Just visualize it and you will begin to see it working for you. See yourself healed, delivered, free, whole, and blessed. I will activate the healing power to be released to you because of your faith. As you reach out by faith and touch what you are, believe for Me to accomplish it in your body, mind, and soul.

SCRIPTURES

Psalm 116:1; Daniel 9:17; Philippians 4:6

HEALING PRAYER

Father, I want to see Your mighty acts demonstrated in my life like never before. Change my hunger for the supernatural to be evident in my life. Reboot me and recharge me by Your Holy Spirit. In Jesus' name, amen.

HEALING CONFESSIONS AND COMMANDS ACTIVATION

I CONFESS AND COMMAND that the healing virtue of Christ is released and transferred to me by faith as I pull on Him.

I CONFESS AND COMMAND that healing is activated in me as I seek the Lord daily for total restoration in every area of my life.

I CONFESS AND COMMAND that I am coming from the back to the forefront.

I CONFESS AND COMMAND that every word curse is nullified and voided by the power of God's Word; and every word curse sent to bring death, sickness, and illness is destroyed, in Jesus' name.

I CONFESS AND COMMAND that I am not subdued or seduced by evil influences and my mental state is healthy. I renounce any mental, eating, physical, and emotional disorders, in Jesus' name.

I CONFESS that I now have faith, which is the substance of things hoped for and the evidence of things not seen (Hebrews 11:1).

I CONFESS AND COMMAND that my emotions will not dictate my physical condition nor will my emotions become an open door to sickness and disease.

DAY 39

MATTHEW 15:21-28 (NIV)

Leaving that place, Jesus withdrew to the region of Tyre and Sidon. A Canaanite woman from that vicinity came to him, crying out, "Lord, Son of David, have mercy on me! My daughter is demon-possessed and suffering terribly." Jesus did not answer a word. So his disciples came to him and urged him, "Send her away, for she keeps crying out after us." He answered, "I was sent only to the lost sheep of Israel." The woman came and knelt before him. "Lord, help me!" she said. He replied, "It is not right to take the children's bread and toss it to the dogs."

"Yes it is, Lord," she said. "Even the dogs eat the crumbs that fall from their master's table." Then Jesus said to her, "Woman, you have great faith! Your request is granted." And her daughter was healed at that moment.

God Honors Your Faith

I will help you. I know what you stand in need of before you ask. Know, My child, that I am more than able to come to your rescue. I am not too far away; I am near and here for you. There is a way to come before Me to receive your request. It is called faith. Faith ignites Me and stirs Me up to answer your prayer request expediently.

When you are lost, My child, I will come to redirect your path so that you will be on the road of faith to your destination. I have the Bread of Life who is My Son Jesus, who has been sent from Heaven for you. This bread is only for those who are Mine, those who are in need of healing and deliverance.

153

There are those who will see Me move for you supernaturally, and they will want crumbs from the bread that is yours, to receive healing for themselves. I am looking for great faith in you. Let me see your faith.

SCRIPTURES

Philippians 2:13; John 6:35

HEALING PRAYER

Lord, examine my heart that there is nothing in it that will displease You and bring disgrace to Your name. Give me meat that I will grow in faith and grace in You. In Jesus' name, amen.

HEALING CONFESSIONS AND COMMANDS ACTIVATION

I CONFESS AND COMMAND that the Father is recognizing faith and He is moving suddenly on my requests made in prayer.

I CONFESS AND COMMAND that I am living and operating under an open heaven and there is nothing withheld from me that God said rightfully belongs to me.

I CONFESS AND COMMAND that the spirit of insanity will not grip my heart and mind; I am walking in faith and total cooperation to the Holy Spirit daily.

I CONFESS AND COMMAND that I am a lender and not a borrower and that I am debt free, in Jesus' name.

I CONFESS AND COMMAND that I will be responsible over my spending; and any debt that I have acquired, I will work toward paying it off and give back what I owe. I will not be stressed out over debt, past invoices, or bills.

I CONFESS AND COMMAND that whatsoever I desire according to God's Word, when I pray, I believe that I have received it by faith; it shall be mine (Mark 11:24).

DAY 40

MATTHEW 15:30 (NIV)
*Great crowds came to him, bringing the lame, the
blind, the crippled, the mute and many others, and
laid them at his feet; and he healed them.*

God Heals All Kinds of Conditions

When you are disabled and unable to move spiritually or physically, know that I will mend every broken bone, restore and replenish the tissue and muscle in your body. I will give you nerves and mobilize your limbs so that you will not be crippled, lame, or paralyzed. I am releasing the miracle power you need to be a testimony and symbol of what your Father can do. There is nothing that surprises Me. Bring anything that you believe is impossible before Me and give Me the chance to show you that I am the God of the impossible.

I know you have heard about what I can do, but may not have witnessed it personally. Get ready to see the winds of miracles blow in your life and those you are praying for. I am speaking from My throne room to where you are. I do not like to see you like this and I hurt to see you experience pain. Cry out to Me to be the muscle relaxer and stress reliever that you stand in need of. I can heal and work miracles in all kinds of situations and conditions. I cannot be proven wrong. I am the God who cannot lie.

SCRIPTURES

Matthew 4:23; Mark 2:1-12; John 5

HEALING PRAYER

I know for sure that You will not leave me in this state or condition. It does not matter what condition I am faced with, You can heal me and anything that seems impossible. Allow me to be touched with Your healing mark. In Jesus' name, amen.

HEALING CONFESSIONS AND COMMANDS ACTIVATION

I CONFESS AND COMMAND that there is nothing too impossible or hard for God to solve, heal, deliver, restore, revive, and mend in my life.

I CONFESS that God can heal all kinds of situations and conditions in my life.

I CONFESS that the Lord blesses me, for I am righteous and not wicked. He surrounds me with unmeasurable favor as with a shield (Psalm 5:12).

I CONFESS AND COMMAND that as I speak by faith, I do not doubt in my heart; and what I prophesy will come to pass, and I have what I prophetically release (Mark 11:23).

I CONFESS AND COMMAND that in the presence of God there is glory, honor, strength, power, and gladness that heals me daily (1 Chronicles 16:27).

I CONFESS AND COMMAND that I am not broken but restored completely by the Word of God that brings personal revival and transformation.

*I will give you the keys of the kingdom of heaven; whatever
you bind on earth will be bound in heaven, and whatever
you loose on earth will be loosed in heaven.*

God Gives Keys to His Gatekeepers

There are things that I have that I want you to have access to, My child. In My house there are many mansions, and if it was not so, My Son Jesus would not have told you. There are glory rooms in My presence, and I desire to give you keys to unlock unlimited access of wisdom, favor, blessing, healing, breakthrough, and miracles. These keys are given to those who are in My Kingdom. Only My children will be given binding and loosing power.

You can prohibit things from happening in your life and permit things. Use the keys of My Kingdom that will frame your world for the better. I am releasing keys of healing, breakthrough, deliverance, and miracles. There are keys of prosperity that will cause you to live in a realm of abundance; it is released only through obedience of My Word and a repentant heart. Keep your heart open and pure. I will teach you by My Spirit with wisdom how to unlock closed doors for your life. I give keys to not only my children who are mature, but also gatekeepers who will pray and intercede for their city, community, church, ministry, region, state, and family.

SCRIPTURES

Matthew 16:19; John 14:2

HEALING PRAYER

Father, give me keys that will allow me access to a realm of resources that will prosper me. Father, You are my Key that will open doors that no man can open and open doors for me that no man can shut. In Jesus' name, amen.

HEALING CONFESSIONS AND COMMANDS ACTIVATION

I CONFESS AND COMMAND that I have been given the keys to the Kingdom by the Spirit of God to access what are my spiritual downloads.

I CONFESS AND COMMAND that the keys of the house of David are extended to me according to Isaiah 22:22, that God will open doors for me that no one can shut and shut doors that no one can open.

I CONFESS AND COMMAND that I am a gatekeeper of the place and territory that the Father has entrusted me with.

I CONFESS AND COMMAND that I have access to hidden riches that are in secret places.

I CONFESS AND COMMAND that I have the Father's overflowing grace and the free gift of righteousness. Therefore, I reign in life as a king through Christ (Romans 5:17).

I CONFESS that as I suffer with Christ I shall reign with Him, and there is nothing withheld from me and those who are in Him.

MATTHEW 17:18-21

Jesus rebuked the demon, and it came out of him; and the child was cured from that very hour. Then the disciples came to Jesus privately and said, "Why could we not cast it out?" So Jesus said to them, "Because of your unbelief; for assuredly, I say to you, if you have faith as a mustard seed, you will say to this mountain, 'Move from here to there,' and it will move; and nothing will be impossible for you. However, this kind does not go out except by prayer and fasting."

God Wants to See Mustard Seed Faith

Do not allow what seems small to cause your faith to be small. I use the foolish things to confound the wise. I come to deliver unto you the formula to receive your miracle and breakthrough today. Cheer up and know that I am not going to cause you to stay ignorant. I will inspire your heart this day to see what you want to impart in your heart. There are enemies of your faith that will cause you to think that I will not move the impossible things. Fasting and prayer has the ability to evict, eradicate, and terminate things that are stubborn and unmovable.

I am the God who can move the unmovable and break the spirit of resistance that comes to restrict you from moving into your inheritance. Mountain-moving faith is given as a seed of faith! The faith required to move mountains is through faith that is activated by your mouth to speak to the impossible. You can move mountains based on the Word of Me in your mouth through faith. Speak to the mountains of sickness, disease, disability, poverty, demons, depression, food disorder, obesity, and any circumstance to be removed now.

SCRIPTURES

Matthew 17:20; Mark 11:23; John 6:33

HEALING PRAYER

Give me the power to slay my giants in my life that I will overcome them. Let the mustard seeds of faith cause me to speak to every mountain of resistance to move them. In Jesus' name, amen.

HEALING CONFESSIONS AND COMMANDS ACTIVATION

I CONFESS AND COMMAND that my mustard-size seed of faith will move the mountains that are in my way.

I CONFESS AND COMMAND that every crossed valley of decision in my life will be straighten and made clear for me to understand.

I CONFESS AND COMMAND that I am not victimized or play the victim; rather, I have total control over my destiny by what I decide to do in Christ daily.

I CONFESS AND COMMAND that supernatural faith is released when I seek the face of the Father daily.

I CONFESS AND COMMAND that I am in Christ Jesus. I do not walk after the flesh but after the things of the Spirit. Therefore, I am liberated and free from condemnation (Romans 8:1).

I CONFESS AND COMMAND that I believe by faith that Jesus is Christ— the Anointed One sent by the Father—and I am born of the spirit and of God who overcame the world (1 John 5:1,4).

MATTHEW 21:22 (NIV)

If you believe, you will receive whatever you ask for in prayer.

God Answers Prayers of Faith

ood morning, My child. I have heard your prayers. Don't lose sight of what you are asking Me to do. Do not get uncomfortable or frustrated that things may not be moving at the pace you desire to see it move. I want you, My dear one, to receive your healing and miracle and restoration in your mind before you see it happen in your life. Your faith will activate your prayers to be released. Heaven will come down as you call it forth to manifest in your life now. Did you know that your angels are looking for employment? Angels listen to My voice that is released through those who are Spirit-filled.

Release your faith through reading the Word and declaring it openly over your situation. I answer to prayers and petitions from those who operate in a realm of faith. Silence the naysayer and those who do not believe or trust My Word. If you believe what you receive in prayer when you ask, then you will see it unfold for you in a unique way. I do the unusual things through a peculiar people. You have been made in My image and after My likeness. Let us work together to see the culture of your life change for the better.

SCRIPTURES

Genesis 1:27; Psalm 103:20; 1 Corinthians 1:27

HEALING PRAYER

My faith will release my prayer requests. Teach me by the Holy Spirit to gain access to what You desire for me to receive that is Your will. In Jesus' name, amen.

HEALING CONFESSIONS AND COMMANDS ACTIVATION

I CONFESS AND COMMAND that faith causes my prayers to be answered quickly.

I CONFESS AND COMMAND that my faith in Christ will not be compromised or frustrated.

I CONFESS AND COMMAND that every bad cycle and habit is broken and that the ways of the Lord is exalted in my life.

I CONFESS AND COMMAND that the prayers of the righteous avail much in my life.

I CONFESS AND COMMAND that God is holy; therefore, I am also holy in all my conduct and manner of living.

I CONFESS AND COMMAND that sickness, disease, disability, and lack is not my portion.

I CONFESS AND COMMAND that greater is He who lives in me than he that is in the world (1 John 4:4).

I CONFESS AND COMMAND that without faith it is impossible to please God. Therefore, I am determined to live by faith so that I will always please Him (Hebrews 11:6).

MARK 5:27-34 (NIV)

When she heard about Jesus, she came up behind him in the crowd and touched his cloak, because she thought, "If I just touch his clothes, I will be healed." Immediately her bleeding stopped and she felt in her body that she was freed from her suffering. At once Jesus realized that power had gone out from him. He turned around in the crowd and asked, "Who touched my clothes?" "You see the people crowding against you," his disciples answered, "and yet you can ask, 'Who touched me?'" But Jesus kept looking around to see who had done it. Then the woman, knowing what had happened to her, came and fell at his feet and, trembling with fear, told him the whole truth. He said to her, "Daughter, your faith has healed you. Go in peace and be freed from your suffering."

God Takes Away Suffering

My beloved, did you know that if you suffer with Christ, you will reign with Him? I know you are feeling terrible, whether it is emotionally, mentally, physically, or even spiritually. I want to take you from that place and mentality that is affecting you. My heart to remove those things comes oftentimes as reminders of pain. Know that I will not cause you to go through or relive any nightmares in the physical and natural. Allow Me to step in and become your Troubleshooter.

I will come remotely, with your permission, to debug and remove the virus of life and sickness. Regardless of the doctor's report or what your body is saying to you day in and day out, I come to relieve your pain and remove the suffering. I will exchange your garment of unbelief with a garment and robe of faith and victory. Trust Me today and allow Me to heal you now. I will free you so that you will live in peace and be affliction-free. I come to wipe out the nightmare and give you a daydream of healing and miracles.

SCRIPTURES

Isaiah 52:12, 58:8, 61:7; Revelation 21:4

HEALING PRAYER

Father, I know You will not allow me to suffer for long. It may feel like it is permanent, but You can remove it permanently. In Jesus' name, amen.

HEALING CONFESSIONS AND COMMANDS ACTIVATION

I CONFESS AND COMMAND that sickness, daily illness, viruses, pain, hurt, trauma, affliction, infirmities, and sufferings are not the will of God and I renounce its work in my life.

I CONFESS AND COMMAND that every pain and suffering bows at the name of Jesus.

I CONFESS AND COMMAND that when I am in pain, God is taking away the pain and wiping away every tear from my eyes.

I CONFESS AND COMMAND that I am in a new season and the old season is passed away.

I CONFESS AND COMMAND that I live a separated life committed to the Lord, and I am like a well-watered garden whose spring waters fail not (Isaiah 58:11).

I CONFESS that Jesus is the heart-mender and fixer and His love wipes away all fear.

I CONFESS AND COMMAND that I am not ignorant of the devil's devices. I am determined each day to walk in love and refuse to permit him to take advantage of me (2 Corinthians 2:10-11).

MARK 9:21-24 (NIV)

Jesus asked the boy's father, "How long has he been like this?"
"From childhood," he answered. "It has often thrown him into
fire or water to kill him. But if you can do anything, take
pity on us and help us." "If you can?" said Jesus. "Everything
is possible for one who believes." Immediately the boy's father
exclaimed, "I do believe; help me overcome my unbelief!"

God Works Through the Impossible

My child, know that the very fact that you woke up this morning declares to the earth that you still have an amazing purpose ahead of you. You are given brand-new mercies each day. Your own awakening has given you a daily commission. Others have died prematurely before their time with the same things that you may be encountering in your life. You are a winner and overcomer. Whether what you may be enduring came through the bloodline, or later in life or contracted it, know that everything is possible for those who believe. Do you believe what I can do?

I do not look at pity or defeat; I look at your ability to believe Me to do the impossible. Your faith is connecting to the impossible. The impossible is the link to your faith to trust Me for what you are praying for, whether your faith is for someone else in need of a miracle. Just decree and declare My Word over that situation and circumstances and you will be in awe of what I will and can do. Give me something to do. Give me the impossible things.

Let Me show you that nothing is too hard or farfetched to handle. Don't take no for answer but yes through My Word.

SCRIPTURES

Lamentations 3:23; Job 22:23

HEALING PRAYER

Father, You are the God of the impossible. You make the impossible possible. You make the ordinary extraordinary. Heal me today so that I may heal others today and tomorrow. In Jesus' name, amen.

HEALING CONFESSIONS AND COMMANDS ACTIVATION

I CONFESS that the God of Heaven answers when I call upon Him.

I CONFESS AND COMMAND that when I pronounce, announce, and speak the name of Jesus that demons tremble.

I CONFESS AND COMMAND that I do not fear, for God is my protector, shield, and body guard. And my body will not be harmed nor my life taken accidentally, purposely, or intentionally.

I CONFESS that I endure hardship as a good warrior of Jesus Christ. I stand firm, for God has given me victory (2 Timothy 2:3).

I CONFESS that God surrounds me with people of like faith that I encourage, help, assist, bless, and push me to be all that I can become in Christ.

I CONFESS AND COMMAND that every spiritual gift in me is operative and working to the glory of the Lord.

I CONFESS that Jesus is not ashamed of me, even when I was ashamed of myself at times. Therefore, I am not ashamed of calling Him my Friend.

MARK 11:22-25 (NIV)

"Have faith in God," Jesus answered. "Truly I tell you, if anyone says to this mountain, 'Go, throw yourself into the sea,' and does not doubt in their heart but believes that what they say will happen, it will be done for them. Therefore I tell you, whatever you ask for in prayer, believe that you have received it, and it will be yours. And when you stand praying, if you hold anything against anyone, forgive them, so that your Father in heaven may forgive you your sins."

God Loves Mountain-Moving Faith

Good day, My child, have faith in Me. What I speak in your hearing today is truth. Did you know that you can speak to impossible and make it possible for you? You can relocate everything that seems impossible to move out of your view. Your words have the capacity and creative power to make that happen in your life. It may seem impossible to do in the condition that you are facing or what you have heard. I know in your life that you have heard that you "can't" or "no" or even it "cannot be done."

Listen to Me and know that what I say to you *can* be done and I say yes and it can be done for those who believe. In prayer, I will hear from heaven and send your answer to the earth. Faith prayers for healing, deliverance, liberty, blessing, and breakthrough are on the other side of the mountain. Do not see from a valley view but see from the mountain view. I am here with you to help you climb the mountain of opposition and speak to the mountain of opportunity to bless you.

SCRIPTURES
Proverbs 4:20; Matthew 17:20; Hebrews 11:6

HEALING PRAYER

Father, I have seen many mountains of doubt that have come to discourage me, but I know that through Your Word that inspires my faith, I can speak the impossible and it will move the impossible. In Jesus' name, amen.

HEALING CONFESSIONS AND COMMANDS ACTIVATION

I CONFESS AND COMMAND that my faith will move mountains of doubt, fear, sickness, poverty, and shame.

I CONFESS that my faith increases daily in the Word of God.

I CONFESS that because of the blood of Jesus, God forgives my sins and cleanses me from unrighteousness (1 John 1:9).

I CONFESS that God's love toward me is unfailing and that faith in me is relocating large oppositions in my life.

I CONFESS that as I abide in Jesus, I will continue to bear much fruit to bless others (John 15:5).

I CONFESS AND COMMAND that I am determined to walk in love and not unforgiveness.

I CONFESS AND COMMAND that I will live by faith and not by sight and allow God to move in my life by faith (2 Corinthians 5:7).

MARK 16:18 (NIV)

They will pick up snakes with their hands; and when they drink deadly poison, it will not hurt them at all; they will place their hands on sick people, and they will get well.

God Protects His People and Heals Them

When you call upon My name in times of trouble, I will come to your heart's cry. I hear you and will protect you from harm. The enemy will come to bring destruction, but I come to bring construction. It is his intent to tear you down and push you down, but my heart is to build you up and push you up higher than before. You may face some dangerous and hazardous encounters in your life that are unbelievable. I can safeguard you and shield you from anything potentially deadly. I will keep you from harm that may be spiritual poison or venomous to endure. I have created you to be a healing agent through the Holy Spirit.

Your hands will be the extension of My hands on the earth to release My power. You will lay hands on the sick and they will recover. It is my heartbeat to see you get well and those you pray for by faith receive their healing. Open yourself up to be used mightily for My glory. I am here to work with you to be the vessel of healing and change that your generation is looking for. The only way this world will see the true and living Jesus is through you as a Christian moving in His power by the Holy Spirit.

SCRIPTURES

Matthew 16:18; Romans 10:3

HEALING PRAYER

Cover me, Father, from unforeseen things that mean me harm and protect me from the fiery darts of the enemy. Heal me and deliver me from those things that come to destroy my destiny. In Jesus' name, amen.

HEALING CONFESSIONS AND COMMANDS ACTIVATION

I CONFESS AND COMMAND that every day my life is covered by the protection of Heaven and God's angelic host.

I CONFESS AND COMMAND that I will fight the good fight of faith. It is a good fight because Jesus Christ already won it and defeated the enemy on my behalf (1 Timothy 6:12).

I CONFESS that God will supply all of my needs according to His riches in glory (Philippians 4:19).

I CONFESS AND COMMAND that I am not weak in faith, regardless of what my body goes through. I consider Jesus who heals my body and gives me the strength to go on daily.

I CONFESS that Jesus destroyed him that had the power of death. Therefore, I do not have to live in bondage to the fear of death (Hebrews 2:14-15).

I CONFESS AND COMMAND that the mountains shall depart and the hills be removed, but God's mercy and kindness do not depart from me. Neither is the covenant of peace removed from me (Isaiah 54:10).

LUKE 4:18 (NIV)

The Spirit of the Lord is on me, because he has anointed me to proclaim good news to the poor. He has sent me to proclaim freedom for the prisoners and recovery of sight for the blind, to set the oppressed free.

God Anoints What He Appoints

I have called you in your mother's womb to do something fantastic in your generation. It may not seem like it when you are faced with many of life ups and downs. When you are in dire need of healing or someone you love is in need of it, you are at times left thinking *what is next.* Death seems like a way out or a solution to ease the pain. I say not so and I remove those negative thoughts. You will not go to an early grave. I have anointed you and smeared my oil on you so that others can smell the fragrance of My glory.

My power is not limited to any geographical place and is not limited by one particular church, person, or organization. I have unlimited power through the Holy Spirit to those who are Mine and are Spirit-filled believers ready to be used for My glory. I have sent My Holy Spirit to anoint those whom I have chosen to preach the good news to those poor in the spirit, to liberate the oppressed and bound, and give sight the blind that they may see Me. I anoint the appointed with the Holy Spirit to do great things in the name of My Son, Jesus Christ. Get ready to smear My grace upon those in need of healing.

SCRIPTURES
Psalm 146:8; John 14:12; 1 John 2:20

HEALING PRAYER

I am Your chosen vessel, Father. Empower me to be more than just effective in my generation, but impactful to change lives. In Jesus' name, amen.

HEALING CONFESSIONS AND COMMANDS ACTIVATION

I CONFESS that the Spirit of God anoints His chosen vessels, which I am glad that He has handpicked me for a great assignment and task.

I CONFESS AND COMMAND that the anointing destroys the yoke that is around my neck that is not of God.

I CONFESS AND COMMAND that the oil of healing is flowing from Christ's head to my body.

I CONFESS AND COMMAND that God has delivered me from the kingdom of darkness and gave me the Kingdom of the Son of His love (Colossians 1:13).

I CONFESS AND COMMAND that I will walk in obedience to the Holy Spirit's voice and obey God by keeping my heart perfect toward Him. The Lord shows Himself strong on my behalf (2 Chronicles 16:9).

I CONFESS AND COMMAND that when I am afflicted or in trouble, I pray and the Lord will deliver me out of all my afflictions (Psalm 34:19; James 5:13).

I CONFESS AND COMMAND that the anointing and oil on my life is authentic and not man-made.

LUKE 4:40 (NIV)

At sunset, the people brought to Jesus all who had various kinds
of sickness, and laying his hands on each one, he healed them.

God's Healing Hands

Are you ready to adventure with Me today? I like when we have personal conversation in prayer that causes your faith to rise. This day I want to know that I will not cause the sun to set without answering what you have sought My face so early for. I don't waste time and I don't want to waste yours either. Time is something I have given to you to maximize. Do not look at what you are experiencing as a setback, but a bridge to crossover to set you up to be a voice of purpose. Things happen in your life to bring about greater glory. My child, understand that the greater the suffering, the greater the authority. With every story there is a glory attached to it, My beloved. My hand is surely and truly upon you. Let me guide you and lead you on this road to healing and total recovery.

This is not something that is reoccurring; I am stopping the schedule of disease and sickness that the enemy has sent your way. I will be your shield of protection. Release unto Me anything in your life that will give the enemy legal access to plague you and oppress you. There will be all types of sickness that you have heard about or even some you would not think you may face yourself. I am the healing balm and come to heal you and set you free by My healing touch. You have been touched by an Angel. I am the Angel with healing in My wings.

SCRIPTURES

Psalm 84:7; Luke 3:5; 1 Corinthians 3:18; Malachi 4:2

HEALING PRAYER

A touch from You, Father, will make what is wrong, right. It's Your healing virtue that is released through faith that activates it. In Jesus' name, amen.

HEALING CONFESSIONS AND COMMANDS ACTIVATION

I CONFESS AND COMMAND that God's healing touch will cure all types of sickness and diseases.

I CONFESS AND COMMAND that I lay aside every weight, which so easily besets me (Hebrews 12:1).

I CONFESS that the healing hands of Jesus will soothe and heal all my problems.

I CONFESS AND COMMAND that the fire of the Holy Spirit will consume everything around me and purify anything that is not God in me.

I CONFESS that the dove of the Holy Spirit will light upon me and reveal that I am too anointed of God to do greater works of ministry.

I CONFESS AND COMMAND that I live the kind of life in God that He intends for me to live by exchanging my thoughts, concepts, ideas, and perspectives for His (Isaiah 55:6-11).

I CONFESS AND COMMAND that my hands are healing hands as well. I can lay hands on the sick and they shall recover and be whole, in Jesus' name.

I CONFESS that God's Word is forever settled in Heaven. I will never change or be modified (Psalm 119:89).

LUKE 6:17-19 (NIV)

He went down with them and stood on a level place. A large crowd
of his disciples was there and a great number of people from all over
Judea, from Jerusalem, and from the coastal region around Tyre and
Sidon, who had come to hear him and to be healed of their diseases.
Those troubled by impure spirits were cured, and the people all tried to
touch him, because power was coming from him and healing them all.

God's Healing Power Is Contagious

What is troubling you and afflicting you, My dear one, I will ward off all and cause them not to come back again. Collaborate with Heaven as I send My angelic host to your side. I will cure you from anything that comes to disrupt My plan and purpose for your life. I will walk in peace and joy this day. The enemy wants to see you totally defeated by things that others may have died from but not so for you. I will reverse the curse and the enemy's verdict over you. I have the last word concerning you.

My power will ooze out of Me as you reach for more of it. I can heal any case that seems unbearable to endure. In My Word, there were those who received healing and their miracle breakthrough just by hearing the healing phenomenon that was done for others. My healing power is radiant like the sun. It can bring light and heat to any damaged part. Do not permit anything to come to steal your peace, joy, and holiness. The throbbing of your pain will be healed by the massaging power of My hand on your life.

SCRIPTURES
Psalm 118:17; Proverbs 6:1-9

HEALING PRAYER

I have no question in my mind about Your miracle working power. It will set me ablaze by the Holy Spirit to release it to those I relate to and pray for. In Jesus' name, amen.

HEALING CONFESSIONS AND COMMANDS ACTIVATION

I CONFESS that God's healing power is contagious enough to bring healing and miracles to those who believe.

I CONFESS AND COMMAND that by my faith it has made me whole.

I CONFESS that Jesus has given me His peace. I do not let my heart be troubled, neither do I walk in fear (John 14:27).

I CONFESS that the Lord takes pleasure in my prosperity. I prosper daily in every area of my life according to His Word (Psalm 35:27).

I CONFESS AND COMMAND that my cup is running and flowing over because of the Holy Spirit out pouring in the presence of God.

I CONFESS AND COMMAND that I open my mouth boldly in faith and make known the gospel of Jesus Christ so others will come unto the Lord and ask what they must do to be saved.

I CONFESS AND COMMAND that I am not just a hearer of the Word of God but also a demonstrator of it.

I CONFESS that I am determined to know Jesus personally each day and experience the power of His resurrection (Philippians 3:10).

LUKE 8:43-44 (NIV)

And a woman was there who had been subject to bleeding for twelve years, but no one could heal her. She came up behind him and touched the edge of his cloak, and immediately her bleeding stopped.

God Holds the Cure to Every Condition

Good morning, My child. I watched you while you slept. I am excited that you are awake. I hope that you are feeling better today than you felt yesterday. I know that there may be things that you have been struggling with for a while and is hard to break. I truly understand. Those things that you want to surrender over to Me, I am willing to take them from you. I want to stop any reoccurring issue or problem that has hindered you.

As you come in agreement with the Word that I speak, you will begin to see circumstances and situations change for you. Deliver those things that have been constant reminders of negativity. Cast those burdens to Me and I will give you rest. This is a brand-new day for you. I release jubilee and favor over you. You are moving in an accelerated pace. Turn over anything and everything that you feel is causing discouragement and pain. I come to relieve you finally. I can cure any illness and heal any disease.

SCRIPTURES

Isaiah 14:3; Psalm 3:5; 1 Peter 5:7

HEALING PRAYER

Father, You are a life saver. Through Jesus' blood I am protected. Whatever I am facing in life, Father, You are here to encourage, console, and inspire me. In Jesus' name, amen.

HEALING CONFESSIONS AND COMMANDS ACTIVATION

I CONFESS that God holds the cure to every disease, sickness, and illness and that is why Jesus bore our sins, sickness, and iniquities.

I CONFESS AND COMMAND that diseases and sicknesses are not the will of God for my life, and I do not receive it, in Jesus' name.

I CONFESS that Jesus is my Lord and the Father has raised Him from the dead. He was my substitute. He is my Savior; satan has no power over my life or over my body, mind, and soul (Philippians 2:11; Romans 10:9-10).

I CONFESS that Jesus is my Healer and satan is the oppressor. God anointed Jesus of Nazareth with the Holy Spirit and with power; He went about doing good and healing all who were oppressed by the devil (Acts 10:38).

I CONFESS that I serve the One whose name is, *"I am the Lord who heals you"* (Exodus 15:26).

I CONFESS that Jesus Christ is the same yesterday and today and forever (Hebrews 13:8).

I CONFESS that Jesus came that I may have life and have it in its entirety and fullness (John 10:10).

Luke 9:11 (NIV)
But the crowds learned about it and followed him. He welcomed them and spoke to them about the kingdom of God, and healed those who needed healing.

God's Healing Kingdom

As you grow in your understanding of who I am, you will see the truth of My Word. There are those who believe that I permit sickness to happen to them to teach them a lesson. That is far from the truth. I heal sickness and disease; ill health is not part of My will. Don't allow false doctrine of healing to cloud your mind. Sickness, disease, and illness is not in Heaven nor is it part of My Kingdom.

When people heard about the miracle power that was demonstrated through Jesus' ministry, people came from all over to receive their personal healing. I give away miracles and healings to those who believe. The spirit of infirmity has the power to cause decay to the mind and body. However, trust in My supernatural intervention that will render unto you what you are in need of. I welcome all who come to Me with their request to be healed and liberated from all their pain. My Kingdom is a healing and miracle-working Kingdom by the Holy Spirit.

SCRIPTURES
2 Peter 3:18; John 14:11; Philippians 1:9

HEALING PRAYER

I want to live in Your supernatural Kingdom. Give me the ability to operate in my gifts and discover what they are to be a blessing to others. In Jesus' name, amen.

HEALING CONFESSIONS AND COMMANDS ACTIVATION

I CONFESS that God's healing Kingdom is in me by the Holy Spirit.

I CONFESS that God desires that I prosper and be in good health (3 John 2).

I CONFESS that my Father is supplying all of my needs according to His riches and glory in Christ Jesus (Philippians 4:19).

I CONFESS that the Lord is my Helper and I will not be afraid of any report that I may hear (Hebrews 13:6).

I CONFESS AND COMMAND according to God's Word that the weak say, I am strong; and I am strong in the Lord (Joel 3:10).

I CONFESS that according to God's Word the "inhabitant will not say I am sick." Therefore, I will not say it either. I will say what God has said in His Word. By His wounds I have been healed (Isaiah 33:24; 1 Peter 2:24).

I CONFESS that in God's healing Kingdom the words I speak have power, and when I speak God's Word I am planting good seed into my life (Luke 8:11).

LUKE 9:42 (NIV)

Even while the boy was coming, the demon threw him to the ground in a convulsion. But Jesus rebuked the impure spirit, healed the boy and gave him back to his father.

God Rebukes Evil Spirits and Restore Health

Guard your heart! Keep yourself free from sin and anything that would be an open door to sin. The enemy is like a roaring lion looking for those who are weak to devour. I will not allow you to fall prey to the devil's tactics and cause you to miss what is due to you. Your healing and deliverance are in your decisions. Your destiny is determined by your decisions. Sickness and disease are not choices that any one chooses; but your actions many times become the consequences you face.

Know that I desire for you, My beloved, to walk freely and stay free. Whom My Son Jesus sets free is free indeed. Do not be tangled or unevenly yoked with unbelievers. Keep yourself whole and pure. There are forces in the earth that will resist your deliverance and keep you from receiving your divine health. I will restore your health and rebuke every evil spirit that comes to you illegally. Whatever bands and bondages come into your life, I am the Chain Breaker! I will break every chain and loose every fetter around your feet.

SCRIPTURES
Proverbs 4:23; 2 Corinthians 3:17, 6:14

HEALING PRAYER

I thank You that I no longer am a product of my past but I will produce Your will for the future. Make clear Your will for my life that will not lose sight of it. In Jesus' name, amen.

HEALING CONFESSIONS AND COMMANDS ACTIVATION

I CONFESS that God will rebuke evil spirit and restore my health to whole.

I CONFESS and know by faith that I will tread upon serpent and scorpions and nothing by any means will harm me.

I CONFESS AND COMMAND that I will hold fast to the confession of God's Word without wavering, for He who promised is faithful (Hebrews 4:14; 10:23).

I CONFESS AND COMMAND that no evil spirits will have no influence in my life and I renounce every work of satan, in Jesus' name.

I CONFESS AND COMMAND I am not weak in faith, so I do not consider my own body above what God has said (Romans 4:19).

I CONFESS AND COMMAND that I don't put any confidence in my flesh, but I put my sole confidence in Jesus and in His Word (Philippians 3:3).

I CONFESS AND COMMAND myself not to waver at the promise of God through unbelief, but I am fully convinced that what He has promised He is also able to perform (Romans 4:20-21).

LUKE 13:10-13 (NIV)

On a Sabbath Jesus was teaching in one of the synagogues, and a woman was there who had been crippled by a spirit for eighteen years. She was bent over and could not straighten up at all. When Jesus saw her, he called her forward and said to her, "Woman, you are set free from your infirmity." Then he put his hands on her, and immediately she straightened up and praised God.

God Can Straighten Out Any Condition

Reflect on your breakthrough each and every day. Make this day count, My child. Don't look at your condition as a "woe is me," or "why me?" Whatever is causing deformity physically in your life, I will come to bring balance and will align what is misaligned. Life does come at times to cripple you and break you down so that you will not function at your full capacity.

Know that I will straighten out and straighten up all types of conditions that may cripple you spiritually and physically. Let Me touch every area that has been plagued by the spirit of infirmity, which causes deformity or disability. I want to straighten out the situation in your life for My glory. It does not matter how long you may have been suffering or battling with something that is not My will or plan for your life. I will deliver and heal you every single time.

SCRIPTURES

Psalm 50:15; Jeremiah 15:21

HEALING PRAYER

Father, allow me to continue to walk on the straight and narrow road. Deliver me from the broad and wide street that leads to destruction. Show me the King's highway. In Jesus' name, amen.

HEALING CONFESSIONS AND COMMANDS ACTIVATION

I CONFESS that that God can straighten out any situation, condition, and circumstance.

I CONFESS that I am not moved by what I feel. I am not moved by what I see. For I "walk by faith, not by sight." I am moved only by what I know and believe in Christ, which is through the Word of God (2 Corinthians 5:7).

I CONFESS that the Word of God is truth (John 17:17).

I CONFESS AND COMMAND that pleasant words are health, healing, and medicine to my bones (Proverbs 16:24).

I CONFESS that God's Word can straighten out everything that is crooked, perverted, and not aligned.

I CONFESS AND COMMAND that I have been called to freedom (Galatians 5:13).

I CONFESS AND COMMAND that I am God's workmanship, created in Christ Jesus (Ephesians 2:10).

LUKE 14:3-4 (NIV)

Jesus asked the Pharisees and experts in the law, "Is it lawful to heal on the Sabbath or not?" But they remained silent. So taking hold of the man, he healed him and sent him on his way.

God Can Heal on Any Day

Awake and arise! Today I want to perform a work in you that you have not seen before. I am breaking the spirit of legalism that comes to keep you bound to the system of men. Where the spirit of Me is present, there is liberty. The spirit of legalism keeps My people from moving in the gifts of the Spirit and also embracing their healing. It does not matter what day is, I can perform a miracle on any day. I am not restricted to man-made order, structures, and laws. I am the God who cannot be defined by man-made rules.

As the Creator of the universe, I set the stars, moon, and sun in place. I have given man times and seasons and there is nothing that can stop Me from breaking the law of the universe to bring forth healing and miracles. The limitations of man do not limit or hold me back from working My power. It is faith that moves Me to work a miracle. A miracle breaks the natural law of science to bring about a lasting result of change. Know, My loved one, that if the devil is threatened by your potential, then can you imagine what he goes through when you are fulfilling your purpose? Let us together torture him with your success and healing breakthrough.

SCRIPTURES
Psalm 77:14; Ephesians 3:20-21

HEALING PRAYER

Father, I thank You for hearing my prayers. Regardless what day or time it is, You work overtime for me. You will move Heaven and earth for me to receive My healing and breakthrough. In Jesus' name, amen.

HEALING CONFESSIONS AND COMMANDS ACTIVATION

I CONFESS that God is not limited to healing me on specific days but can heal me anytime I may be sick.

I CONFESS that I am a new creation in Christ Jesus. Old things have passed away and all things have become new and all things belong to God (2 Corinthians 5:17).

I CONFESS AND COMMAND that I am complete in Jesus, who is the head of all rule and authority (Colossians 2:10).

I CONFESS AND COMMAND that I am a believer and all things are possible to me (Mark 9:23).

I CONFESS AND COMMAND that greater is He who is in me than he (the defeated one) that is in the world (who is the author of sickness) (Luke 13:16; 1 John 4:4; Acts 10:38).

I CONFESS that I am an overcomer and I overcome by the blood of the Lamb and the word of my testimony (1 John 4:4; Revelation 12:11).

I CONFESS that I am submitted to His Word, and the devil flees from me because I resist him in the supreme authority of Jesus' name (Mark 16:17; James 4:7).

LUKE 17:12-15 (NIV)

As he was going into a village, ten men who had leprosy met him. They stood at a distance and called out in a loud voice, "Jesus, Master, have pity on us!" When he saw them, he said, "Go, show yourselves to the priests." And as they went, they were cleansed. One of them, when he saw he was healed, came back, praising God in a loud voice.

God Heals Your Mind, Body, and Soul

Good day, My child. Do not take for granted the blessing that has been allotted to you. There are people who are in a worse state and condition than you. Do not complain or murmur over what it looks like. I want to change your natural lenses so that you can see from my scope and view. I do not see from how mere men see things. I see things as in their complete work. I see things from the finished work. In other words, if you are asking Me for healing in your mind, body, and soul, see yourself healed by faith and walk in victory over sickness.

Know that I see you in a transformed state. If you pray for healing, I see from My lenses that you are already healed and it is my heart for you to see the way I see things. Do not see from the condition of where you are currently, see from where you want to be tomorrow. Let Me cleanse the areas of your heart so I can come and live there by My Spirit. Rest in My love and peace, My child. Praise Me with a loud voice so those who hear will know that I have done a new thing in your life.

SCRIPTURES
Matthew 21:22, 10:32; Mark 11:24; John 14:13

HEALING PRAYER

Father, make me over and renew within me a new heart. Cleanse me inside and outside. Remove any spot or blemish that isn't pleasing to Your sight. In Jesus' name, amen.

HEALING CONFESSIONS AND COMMANDS ACTIVATION

I CONFESS AND COMMAND that my body, mind, and soul are healed, in Jesus' name.

I CONFESS AND COMMAND that no weapon formed against me shall prosper, for righteousness is of the Lord (Isaiah 54:17; 1 Corinthians 1:30).

I CONFESS AND COMMAND that nothing evil or wicked will happen to me, neither shall any demonic plague, sickness, or disease come near me (Psalm 91:10).

I CONFESS AND COMMAND that my mind is at peace and I refuse any confusion, fear of dying, or stress to overtake me.

I CONFESS AND COMMAND that my body is healed and it is stronger than ever before.

I CONFESS AND COMMAND that my soul is at ease and there is settling in my heart.

I CONFESS that Jesus gave me authority over the power of the enemy, and nothing shall hurt me (Mark 16:17; Luke 10:19).

Luke 18:42-43 (NIV)

Jesus said to him, "Receive your sight; your faith has healed you."
Immediately he received his sight and followed Jesus, praising
God. When all the people saw it, they also praised God.

God Restore Sight to the Blind

Arise, My child, and gaze upon what is before you. I want to remove the blinders that are blocking your vision of what I am capable to do for you. As you seek My Word today, I will open your eyes to see beyond what is present. I will give sight to the blind and be a guiding light to those need with direction by the Holy Spirit. What you cannot see, I will remove the scales that are placed by the enemy. My Word reveals the truth to those who pray for their eyes of understanding to be enlightened. As you ask Me to open your spiritual eyes, know that My Spirit will become a magnifying glass that will enlarge your view.

Understand today that I will give you 20/20 vision. It is My desire to sharpen your vision and give you keen sight as an eagle. Restoration will come to those who want their eyes opened to receive their healing. As I have given sight many times to the blind in My Word. I will give sight to those who are living in darkness. I will not have you or anyone I call Mine walking in ignorance. You will know and see the truth, and it will make you see and whole.

SCRIPTURES

Isaiah 61:1; Romans 8:14; John 14:26,
16:13; 2 Corinthians 2:11

HEALING PRAYER

Heavenly Father, I thank You that I no longer will live in darkness and be blindsided by the enemy. Open my eyes wide so I will never be deceived; I will walk in my personal healing. In Jesus' name, amen.

HEALING CONFESSIONS AND COMMANDS ACTIVATION

I CONFESS that God will open my spiritual eyes to see that there is more with me than against me.

I CONFESS AND COMMAND that I do not return evil for evil, but on the contrary, blessing that I may obtain blessing (1 Peter 3:9).

I CONFESS that God will restore sight to the blind and open the eyes of those who are spiritually blind and in need of the truth.

I CONFESS that I forgive freely as God has forgiven me. I do not hold anything against anyone (Mark 11:25; Ephesians 4:32).

I CONFESS AND COMMAND that I hold my peace and tongue from evil. I shun away from evil and do well. I seek peace and pursue it. I will love life and see good days in the Kingdom (1 Peter 3:10-11).

I CONFESS AND COMMAND that I have a happy heart and that does my heart glad like medicine (Proverbs 17:22).

I CONFESS AND COMMAND that I have cast all my cares on the Lord for He cares for me. I refuse to worry about anything (1 Peter 5:7).

JOHN 5:5-9 (NKJV)

Now a certain man was there who had an infirmity thirty-eight years. When Jesus saw him lying there, and knew that he already had been in that condition a long time, He said to him, "Do you want to be made well?" The sick man answered Him, "Sir, I have no man to put me into the pool when the water is stirred up; but while I am coming, another steps down before me." Jesus said to him, "Rise, take up your bed and walk." And immediately the man was made well, took up his bed, and walked. And that day was the Sabbath.

God's Word Will Make You RISE!

Rise and shine, My child. Attend to My Word this day. Allow My promises to be like a friendly reminder of what I desire to do for My covenant people. I know what you are dealing with internally and I am not pleased to see you like this. Every day has challenges, but know that you can overcome them one step at a time. I will come with a strategic plan to change the outcome for you. Do not allow fatigue, laziness, the spirit of depression, infirmity, disability, or sickness keep you from fulfilling your dream.

What obstacles are in your way that are keeping you from diving head first into the purpose that I have for you? You are the only one who can set the limitations and restrictions on your life. Let me remove those boundaries and mental blocks that restrain you from rising. Are you waiting for others to put you in the race? Arise today and make up your mind to be the winner I have created you to become. Do not miss your season of breakthrough.

Arise and walk into your purpose. Be healed and delivered from the restrictors in your life.

SCRIPTURES

2 Thessalonians 3; Job 36:16; John 5:8

HEALING PRAYER

Father, I will not stay in the same condition that I once stayed in. Give me the word to take up my bed and to walk, and I will obey. In Jesus' name, amen.

HEALING CONFESSIONS AND COMMANDS ACTIVATION

I CONFESS that God' Word will bring life to me and cause me to rise.

I CONFESS AND COMMAND that I have the strength of an ox.

I CONFESS AND COMMAND that healing is the children's bread.

I CONFESS AND COMMAND that I serve the Lord my God, and He blesses my bread, and my water, and He has taken sickness away from me. For Jesus Himself, took my infirmities and bare my sicknesses away (Exodus 23:25; Matthew 8:17).

I CONFESS AND COMMAND that I will live and not fall asleep in death. I declare that I have more to do in this earth to fulfill my God-given destiny.

I CONFESS AND COMMAND that Christ is my Passover and was sacrificed for me. All sickness and death must pass over me and my household now, in Jesus' name (Exodus 12; 1 Corinthians 5:7).

I CONFESS AND COMMAND that I am blessed above all people. The Lord has taken away from me all sickness (Deuteronomy 7:14-15).

DAY 59

JOHN 9:1-7 (NIV)

*As he went along, he saw a man blind from birth. His disciples
asked him, "Rabbi, who sinned, this man or his parents, that he
was born blind?" "Neither this man nor his parents sinned," said
Jesus, "but this happened so that the works of God might be displayed
in him. As long as it is day, we must do the works of him who sent
me. Night is coming, when no one can work. While I am in the
world, I am the light of the world." After saying this, he spit on the
ground, made some mud with the saliva, and put it on the man's
eyes. "Go," he told him, "wash in the Pool of Siloam" (this word
means "Sent"). So the man went and washed, and came home seeing.*

God's Healing Pool

My child, I like to show off My power in usual circumstances. It allows
Me to prove people wrong who are wise and proud. I know, My child,
you have many questions in your mind about life and things that happen that
may not be in your control. I know all things and everything is ordained by
Me. There are sicknesses and infirmities caused by sin and disobedience. If a
person sows to the flesh, then he or she will reap corruption. Moreover, in My
Word it says that the wages of sin is death, but the gift of God is eternal life.

Keep yourself free from sin and walk in My ways. Follow the direction
of the Holy Spirit. He will not lead you onto the wrong path. Your life is
important to Me, and it is My passion to see you excel in life and prosper.
There are conditions that people are born with that have nothing to do with

sin. One may ask why this person has to suffer or were they born this way? But everything is done on purpose to bring Me glory so that I will work a miracle. There is a place where I send those who I will use to bring Me glory through signs, wonders, and miracles.

SCRIPTURES

Romans 6:23; John 9:1-3

HEALING PRAYER

I want to jump into the river that is flowing with healing. Your Word is a healing pool that You send to those, Father, who need to be cleansed and washed. In Jesus' name, amen.

HEALING CONFESSIONS AND COMMANDS ACTIVATION

I CONFESS that God's healing pool will bring healing and miracles to those who believe and dip into it by His Word.

I CONFESS AND COMMAND that I will fear the Lord and my days will be prolonged as I keep my heart with all diligence, for out of it flows the issues of life (Proverbs 4:23; 10:27).

I CONFESS AND COMMAND that my desire is only of the Lord; hope in Him is a tree of life. I fear the Lord as my fountain of life. I have a sound heart, which is life for my body (Proverbs 13:12; 14:27,30).

I CONFESS AND COMMAND that the will of the Lord is done in my life and on earth as it is in Heaven. There is no sickness in Heaven; therefore, I am not sick on this earth. Jesus is in me and His life flows in me. As He was in the world so am I in this world.

I CONFESS AND COMMAND that I am healthy as Jesus was full and healthy upon this earth (Matthew 6:10; Galatians 2:20; 1 John 4:17).

I CONFESS that Jesus destroyed the works of the devil, which were bodily infirmities, diseases, illnesses, sicknesses, and disabilities; therefore, all the works of the devil upon my body are destroyed and I have perfect health in Jesus Christ (Matthew 8:17; 1 John 3:8; Acts 10:38).

JOHN 10:10 (NIV)

The thief comes only to steal and kill and destroy; I have come that they may have life, and have it to the full.

God Offers Eternal Life

One of the greatest days that I recall, was when you were born, My child. I rejoiced and danced over you because a star was being born into the earth. You were exactly how I envisioned and created you to be. It is my desire to see you walk in a measure of godly success. I was also there when you took your first step, formulated your first words, and even made your own decisions. As you grow and mature, life has given you a run for your money. You were tested, tempted, and challenged to make some hard decisions that will make you or break you.

There was someone else there who was not so happy that you were born. You were on the devil's hit list. He comes to harass you and to bring you down. The devil is not going to play fair. But know, My child, that I will not allow him to get the upper hand. My hand is surely upon you as you trust Me to lead you and fight your battles. He is no match for Me. He will not take you out. He can't offer you anything but death; but I offer you eternal life and life that is full of enjoyment in Me. Learn and live.

SCRIPTURES

Isaiah 59:19; 1 Peter 5:8; Acts 17:11

HEALING PRAYER

You have delivered me in the time of trouble. You have shielded me from the wiles of the devil. I am in Your hands and am safe. In Jesus' name, amen.

HEALING CONFESSIONS AND COMMANDS ACTIVATION

I CONFESS that I have eternal life in Christ and I am a joint heir.

I CONFESS AND COMMAND that I am saved and I am walking in obedience to the will of God on my life.

I CONFESS AND COMMAND sickness and disease will not bind me up or hold me down.

I CONFESS AND COMMAND that I will be in peace and be continually healed and free from every type of distressing bodily disease. I will not be seized with alarm or struck with fear, but I will keep on believing God (Mark 5:34-36).

I CONFESS that my God has declared that He will restore me to great health and heal all my wounds; He who promised is faithful and just to keep His Word (Jeremiah 30:17; Hebrews 10:23).

I CONFESS AND COMMAND that my salvation will not be taken from me; I will protect it.

I CONFESS AND COMMAND that my health is springing forth rapidly. My healing is suddenly appearing (Isaiah 58:8).

JOHN 14:12-14 (NLT)

I tell you the truth, anyone who believes in me will do the same works I have done, and even greater works, because I am going to be with the Father. You can ask for anything in my name, and I will do it, so that the Son can bring glory to the Father. Yes, ask me for anything in my name, and I will do it!

God's Mighty Acts Demonstrated

Hasn't it been said in My Word that those who are mine will do greater works than Jesus, My Son? Because He is seated at My right hand of power, My child, now you have been commissioned by the Holy Spirit to demonstrate the power of healing, deliverance, miracles, signs, and wonders to those in need of His unique touch. There are no limitations of what you are able and capable of doing by faith in Me. Don't allow doubt, unbelief, or fear to take residence in your mind, heart, or spirit.

You are to be a healing agent and miracle advocate of the Holy Spirit. My power is available for those who believe in My Son, Jesus. I tell you the truth, My beloved, that the quantity and quality of miracles will be performed through a vessel of pure motives, compassion, and faith to get it done. Get ready for the ride of your life. Rise up and heal. Rise up and deliver. Arise, My child, and work miracles here and now. Rise up and be like Christ in your generation.

SCRIPTURES
John 14:12; Mark 16:19; Acts 7:55-56

HEALING PRAYER

Father, You have chosen me for a special assignment. It will take great faith to accomplish this task. Equip me by Your Holy Spirit and educate me by Your Word that I will not fail in my endeavors. In Jesus' name, amen.

HEALING CONFESSIONS AND COMMANDS ACTIVATION

I CONFESS that God's supernatural power flows through me by the Holy Spirit.

I CONFESS AND COMMAND that the fruit of the Spirit is evident in my life and the gifts of the Spirit are manifesting.

I CONFESS AND COMMAND that I will not lack anything that God has promised me each day.

I CONFESS AND COMMAND that I am in good condition and that my mind and retention is sharp each day.

I CONFESS AND COMMAND that my God-given destiny is not changed, altered, or delayed.

I CONFESS AND COMMAND that I will dream the dreams of Heaven and I am moving in the timetable of the Lord for my life.

I CONFESS AND COMMAND that every prophetic promise spoken over my life is yes and not denied.

JOHN 11:25-26

Jesus said to her, "I am the resurrection and the life. He who believes in Me, though he may die, he shall live. And whoever lives and believes in Me shall never die. Do you believe this?"

God Gives Resurrection Life

There are those who will transition from this life into the other life. They will not have the opportunity that is allotted each day to believe in Jesus Christ, My Son, and receive eternal life. Life in Heaven is greater than just a personal healing, deliverance, and miracle. It is a precious and special privilege to receive the gift of eternal life. Live life abundantly in Christ right now on earth until it's your time to see Him face to face. You will not be cast off or cast away. However, there will be those, My child, who will hear those haunting words from Christ in that day, "I never knew you; depart from Me, you who practice lawlessness!" (Matthew 7:23).

Know that I sent My Son to the earth with a great assignment and tremendous proposition for those who will accept, believe, and receive Him into their hearts. He is the resurrection and the life. Those who will believe on His name will live; and when that time comes when their name is called, they will live and never perish. I know this reality is hard to absorb, that is why it's very important that My message of the Gospel is spread, heralded, and preached to unbelievers.

SCRIPTURES

Matthew 7:21-23; John 17:3

HEALING PRAYER

I am grateful to have received You into my heart, Jesus. I will not take for granted this awesome opportunity to know You and receive You into my heart. Father, allow me open doors so I can share with others what I have received at salvation. In Jesus' name, amen.

HEALING CONFESSIONS AND COMMANDS ACTIVATION

I CONFESS AND COMMAND that I will live a life of divine happiness, peace, and joy in the Spirit.

I CONFESS AND COMMAND that the Holy Spirit is my Counselor, Consultant, Advocate, and Advisor.

I CONFESS AND COMMAND that I will not miss my divine season of promotion and elevation.

I CONFESS AND COMMAND that the windows of Heaven are opening over me due to my consistent ability to work godly principles of sowing, tithing, and seeding into fertile ground.

I CONFESS AND COMMAND that I am alert, aware, and coherent in the Spirit.

I CONFESS AND COMMAND that I walk in Holy Spirit boldness, and fear will not grip my heart.

I CONFESS AND COMMAND my spiritual eyes to have 20/20 vision in the realm of the Spirit and that I will not lose sight of what I am called to do and become.

I CONFESS that I am the righteousness of Christ and that everything I am connected to will prosper.

Acts 3:6-7 (NIV)

*Then Peter said, "Silver or gold I do not have, but what I
have I give you. In the name of Jesus Christ of Nazareth,
walk." Taking him by the right hand, he helped him up, and
instantly the man's feet and ankles became strong.*

God Is Able to Heal Anyone

My child, understand how blessed you are to be here today to spend time with Me. Oh how I love to see you rise daily with a plan to seek My face for direction and understanding. The fear of the Lord is the beginning of wisdom, and I want to release daily wisdom that will make you successful. I want to heal you and bring you to a place where you can live to enjoy the blessings from Me. Heaven is a treasure box of blessings, and I want to give you the keys.

There are those who believe they can buy their way into Heaven with their wealthy or rich status. And there are those who believe they can make it into Heaven because of their status, title, worldly position, and credibility. Not at all is the case. It takes a righteous heart that believes in Jesus and would give up worldly fame, possessions, and fortunes to follow Christ. Money and fame can't heal cancer, blood disease, sickness, illness, all kinds of disabilities, and the like. I am the only One who can and is willing to heal and create nothing out of something. I will give strength to the lame and sight to the blind and wholeness to the lost. I can do the impossible!

SCRIPTURES
Deuteronomy 7:6; Psalm 110:1; Proverbs 9:10

HEALING POWER

Father, You are the Source of my personal healing and transformation. I will not count on worldly things to bring healing or happiness. You are the only Source. In Jesus' name, amen.

HEALING CONFESSIONS AND COMMANDS ACTIVATION

I CONFESS that God is able to heal those in need; and when I am standing in a need of divine breakthrough, He comes through for me every time.

I CONFESS AND COMMAND that I am an overcomer and more than a conqueror in Christ Jesus.

I CONFESS AND COMMAND that I am highly favored of the Lord and He calls me His friend.

I CONFESS that the grace of our Lord Jesus Christ, that though He was rich, yet for my sake He became poor, that I through His poverty might be rich (2 Corinthians 8:9).

I CONFESS AND COMMAND that each day as I seek the face of God that the Lord shall increase me more and more; and not only me, but my children and children's children (Psalm 115:14).

I CONFESS and declare that I am not under any witchcraft prayer or sorcery, but I am liberated by the power of God.

I CONFESS AND COMMAND that I am a healing vessel and that God has given me a grace by the Spirit to heal the sick and cure the disease.

ACTS 3:16 (NIV)

By faith in the name of Jesus, this man whom you see and know was made strong. It is Jesus' name and the faith that comes through him that has completely healed him, as you can all see.

God Completes the Healing Process

Be strong! I know you are weak. Whether it's physically, mentally, or spiritually, but know that I will come to be your spiritual protein shake to give you a boost. Trust in the process of faith and what accompanies it, which is healing. By faith in the name of My Son Jesus, you will receive your divine strength and miracle. There is no special formula or method, but simply have faith. I am looking for faith in those who desire to see My supernatural power demonstrated in their own lives and in others.

I don't do a half job when it comes to healing someone. I did not do a half job creating you, My child. You were birthed out of My own interest, desire, and love. You were hidden with Me before the foundations of the world. You were there with Me when I created the universe and the host of them. I am the same One who can create a miracle for you if you are in need of it. My arms are not too short to touch you and complete the healing in your life. Healing requires rest. So rest in My presence and take it one day at a time.

SCRIPTURES

Romans 3:22; Ephesians 6:10

HEALING PRAYER

*Thank You, Father, for finishing the work that You have started in me.
I know and understand that I possess the Holy Spirit to finish what You
have called me to finish in my generation. In Jesus' name, amen.*

HEALING CONFESSIONS AND COMMANDS ACTIVATION

I CONFESS AND COMMAND that when I am in need of healing that it is already done and finished at Calvary's cross.

I CONFESS that the Lord is able to make all grace (every favor and earthly blessing) come to me in abundance, so that I may always be self-sufficient (possessing enough to require no aid or support and furnished in abundance for every good work and charitable donation) (2 Corinthians 9:8).

I CONFESS that the Lord blesses me in every way, and I break every curse that will try to steal my joy.

I CONFESS that as I am meek in Christ I will inherit the earth and shall delight myself in the abundance of peace, wealth, health, and good welfare (Psalm 37:11).

I CONFESS that my life is sold out to the Lord and He has purchased me with His blood.

I CONFESS AND COMMAND that I shall pray for those who despitefully use me, bless those who curse me, love those who hate me, and help those in need.

I CONFESS AND COMMAND that healing and deliverance is my Kingdom inheritance.

Acts 9:33-34

There he found a man named Aeneas, who was paralyzed and had been bedridden for eight years. "Aeneas," Peter said to him, "Jesus Christ heals you. Get up and roll up your mat." Immediately Aeneas got up.

God Heals the Paralyzed

Good morning, My shining star. It is my desire to open the curtain of a dark room and cause my light to shine through. The spirit of depression and oppression is twins that come to confuse you to which one is which. I come to break and separate the two. There are agents from hell that will keep you crippled and paralyzed. I come with the crutch of My hand that will cause you to stand back on your feet again. Your setback may seem like a failure on the surface, My loved one, but it is actually a setup for your comeback. Many have counted you out and even you have counted yourself out when you were knocked down. This is not true.

I come as your Referee to see the technical fouls that the enemy did to you while you were in the fight. You are a champion! You are an overcomer! You are a winner! There is still a fight in you. Do not give in or cave in, My child. Yes, the hits of life were hard punches and the enemy tried to kick you while you were down. I have come to bring healing to your paralyzed condition. I come to check your spiritual vital signs and see if you are ready to get back in the game. Rest for a while as the blood pressure of Jesus is transferred to heal every condition and disease.

SCRIPTURES
Matthew 9; John 5; Romans 8:37

HEALING PRAYER

I am the righteousness of Christ. I am an overachiever! I will not buckle or fail. Lord God, give me the strength to win every fight. In Jesus' name, amen.

HEALING CONFESSIONS AND COMMANDS ACTIVATION

I CONFESS AND COMMAND that I will not be hindered by sin or unforgiveness.

I CONFESS AND COMMAND that the power of darkness is shattered by the power of the Kingdom of light.

I CONFESS AND COMMAND that God will heal me when I am paralyzed by my decisions.

I CONFESS that I will honor the Lord with my substance and with the first fruits of all my increase.

I CONFESS AND COMMAND that my house will be filled with plenty and my presses shall burst out with new wine (Proverbs 3:9-10).

I CONFESS AND COMMAND that sin and any demonic forces against me, in Jesus' name, will not cripple me.

I CONFESS AND COMMAND that I am blessed coming in and blessed when going out.

I CONFESS AND COMMAND that I will soar like an eagle and God is renewing my strength.

How God anointed Jesus of Nazareth with the Holy Spirit and power, and how he went around doing good and healing all who were under the power of the devil, because God was with him.

God Heals the Oppressed, Depressed, and Possessed

You are not under construction but a spiritual building with beautiful stones and materials built to last. You are a temple that has not been constructed by men's hands but by Mine only. I have orchestrated you as a great masterpiece of mine. You are like fine china showcased behind glass that others admire. I have built you to last and will recall any pieces to be remanufactured. I created you as an original, and you will not leave this earth a copy. You were strategically and methodically carved out. I am proud to see what you have become.

Your potential and the gifts you discover will marvel many. You are a unique vessel that even the powers of hell fear. Why do they fear? You were created in My image and according to My likeness. When I was done creating you, I said to Myself, "What a great gift, creation, and being this person will be." With this in mind, I built your body to house a powerful Source and Person called the Holy Spirit. He will help you to heal the sick, raise the dead, give sight to the blind, cure all kinds of disease, and walk in the fruit of the Spirit. Make this day count, do something good, and heal those who need My healing touch.

SCRIPTURES

Genesis 1:25; Galatians 5:16-26; 1 Peter 2:5

HEALING PRAYER

You free me from the residue of the past. Father, You removed the nightmares of evil. Thank You for being My protector. I break every evil spirit and power that tries to overtake me. You are my Shield, Father, that wards off every fiery dart and speedy bullet of death. In Jesus' name, amen.

HEALING CONFESSIONS AND COMMANDS ACTIVATION

I CONFESS that God heals me and delivers me from any spirit of oppression, depression, and obsession.

I CONFESS AND COMMAND that I am free from any ungodly soul tie that is not healthy and profitable for my spiritual maturity.

I CONFESS AND COMMAND that I will not be tormented by demon spirits, the spirit of infirmities, and illnesses and that Jesus comes to cast out every demonic spirit around me and heal every sickness.

I CONFESS that I am convinced and sure that He who has begun a good work in me will continue until the day of Jesus Christ, developing, cultivating, perfecting, and bringing me to full completion (Philippians 1:6).

I CONFESS AND COMMAND that I will not fall victim to the enemy plans to overwork me and stress me out physically, mentally, and spiritually.

I CONFESS that the Lord has taken my griefs, sorrow, sicknesses, weaknesses, and distresses and carried my pains and hurts away. Jesus was wounded for my transgression, bruised for my guilt and iniquities; the chastisement needed for my peace and well-being was upon Jesus, and by His stripes I am healed and made whole, in Jesus' name.

ACTS 14:8-10 (NIV)

In Lystra there sat a man who was lame. He had been that way from birth and had never walked. He listened to Paul as he was speaking. Paul looked directly at him, saw that he had faith to be healed and called out, "Stand up on your feet!" At that, the man jumped up and began to walk.

God Heals the Crippled, Lame, and Disabled

Be confident today, My child. Don't let your faith be shaken by what you may be feeling, hearing, and witnessing. Life has a plan to make you or break you. I have a better plan to make you and cause you to break through the chaos of life. I come to bring you a flawless victory over things that have been flaws. I turn your attention to Me and seeking My presence for answers. I know what is next and what is up ahead. Take the binoculars of life and gaze into those things I desire for you to focus on.

At times, you may have to adjust one lens after another to understand with clarity and precision. I will show you people, places, and things that come to immobilize you and stunt your growth process by the Holy Spirit. Stand up tall and with assurance that your faith alliance is with Me and not in man. I know that life's walk can cause your legs and feet to be feeble at times. I will come to be your Stabilizer, Splint, Cast, and Bandage that will keep things in place for proper healing and growth. Release your faith, which is required to give you the bounce-back. Hear the word of healing today and the directives to stand up on your feet and walk.

SCRIPTURES

Ezekiel 2:1; Psalm 118:8, 146:3; Acts 26:16

HEALING PRAYER

When I am not looking or feeling my best Father, Your Holy Spirit mirror shows me the lion reflection when at times I feel vulnerable as a kitten. You do not see me as people see me. Release the roar in me and not the meow that others hear. In Jesus' name, amen.

HEALING CONFESSIONS AND COMMANDS ACTIVATION

I CONFESS AND COMMAND that I will not be crippled, lame, disabled, or dysfunctional.

I CONFESS AND COMMAND that every member of my body is working in perfect harmony with its original design.

I CONFESS AND COMMAND that I am gratefully praising the Lord each day and I do not forget all of God's benefits toward me. He forgives all my iniquities and heals all my diseases. He redeems my life from the pit and corruption. He beautifies, dignifies, and crowns me with lovingkindness and tender mercy.

I CONFESS that I attend to God's Word and submit to His saying daily by the Holy Spirit. I will keep God's Word in my view and in the center of my heart. His Word is life to me and healing to my whole body (Proverbs 4:20-22).

I CONFESS AND COMMAND that my destiny is not changed, altered, or delayed.

I CONFESS that God has not given me a spirit of timidity or fear. He has given me a spirit of power and of love and of a calm disposition, a well-balanced mind, discipline, soberness, and self-control in Him (2 Timothy 1:7).

ACTS 19:11-12 (NIV)

God did extraordinary miracles through Paul, so that even handkerchiefs and aprons that had touched him were taken to the sick, and their illnesses were cured and the evil spirits left them.

God Performs the Extraordinary

There are strange things that happen that you may not be able to understand or wrap your mind around. A person who is strange or even different does not imply that they are demonic or ungodly. I am the God who does unusual things and I have a good habit of blowing people's minds and expectations. That is what I call a miracle or a supernatural intervention at work. I am in the business of taking the ordinary and putting My own unique touch on it and making it extraordinary.

Throughout My Word I have used ordinary people to do extraordinary things for My glory. Faith activates the extraordinary by the Holy Spirit. There is nothing too hard for Me or anything I have not seen before. Remember, My child, I am the Creator and nothing takes me by surprise. I love doing extraordinary things through those who will allow Me. This is not magic or hocus-pocus. It is the raw power of the Holy Spirit revealing Christ's power over darkness, sickness, and all diseases. No magic or black art can stand against the power of My Kingdom and work of the Holy Spirit. Are you ready to be that willingly vessel to release My glory?

SCRIPTURES
Genesis 1:1; Isaiah 28:21

HEALING POWER

Father, You performed miracles in the past and still work miracles today. Father, put Your super on my natural and make what is ordinary, extraordinary. In Jesus' name, amen.

HEALING CONFESSIONS AND COMMANDS ACTIVATION

I CONFESS that God will use me for His glory as I obey His Word and attend to His voice.

I CONFESS AND COMMAND that I will do the extraordinary in my life for His glory.

I CONFESS and declare that this is my new season and it will not be hindered by anyone, including myself and those with whom I am related.

I CONFESS that God gives power to me when I am weary and faint.

I CONFESS that God increases upon me daily strength and spiritual medicine by His living Word.

I CONFESS that I will wait upon the Lord each day as He renews my power and strength.

I CONFESS that God will lift me up with wings of strength and raise me as an eagle.

I CONFESS AND COMMAND my body to run and not be weary.

I CONFESS AND COMMAND that I shall not faint or become drained or tired in the spirit.

ROMANS 8:11 (NIV)

And if the Spirit of him who raised Jesus from the dead is living in you, he who raised Christ from the dead will also give life to your mortal bodies because of his Spirit who lives in you.

God's Spirit Renews, Refreshes, and Revives

My child, do you know the greatness that you possess? Are you aware of what you have been created to accomplish here and now on earth? I am not sure you truly understand and can fathom the magnitude of the potential that lies within you. You have been marked before the worlds were framed by faith through My mouth what you can fulfill in your lifetime. You have been created to be a chamber of the Holy Spirit. Know that your body has a greater responsibility than just an outer shell. You were not created to be an egg but an outer shell that within it contains the most powerful element and personality—the Spirit of God.

The same Spirit that raised Jesus My Beloved Son from death dwells in you. Do you realize that My life-giving Spirit came to live in you at the time of salvation? What a remarkable discovery. You possess the ability to live and to give life to those who are in need of a renewable, refreshing revitalization. The immortal, eternal Spirit comes to quicken and give life to your mortal body. Stay connected and partner with the Holy Spirit to see powerful life-changing and life-altering results in your life.

SCRIPTURES
Psalm 33:9; Romans 8:11

HEALING PRAYER

Renew me, Father! Awake me from sleep, and by Your Spirit don't allow me to fall asleep in my grave. Resurrect me that I may be the vessel of power to bring You glory. In Jesus' name, amen.

HEALING CONFESSIONS AND COMMANDS ACTIVATION

I CONFESS that God's Spirit will renew, refresh, revive, and empower me daily.

I CONFESS AND COMMAND that even though I have a physical body, I will not carry on warfare according to the flesh, using mere human weapons (2 Corinthians 10:3-4).

I CONFESS AND COMMAND that I will not walk in fear, anxiety, or take upon myself false burdens.

I CONFESS AND COMMAND the spirit of death will not come near my tent, dwelling, household, or life; Jesus is the Passover.

I CONFESS AND COMMAND that I will frame my world by faith with positive thoughts, words, and with biblical concepts and truth.

I CONFESS AND COMMAND that I will speak life daily over myself and those I love.

I CONFESS that God is fanning the flame and the gifts of God inside me.

I CONFESS that God is stirring up the gifts inside me to raise me up to bless my generation.

ROMANS 8:26 (NIV)

In the same way, the Spirit helps us in our weakness. We do not know what we ought to pray for, but the Spirit himself intercedes for us through wordless groans.

God Intercedes for You

I use your weakness as a platform of strength. I use the weak to confound the strong things. Know that I love to make an example out of things that the enemy tries to bring embarrassment and shame to. It is my heart to put the enemy to shame and embarrassment. You are one of a kind and belong to Me. I have sent the Holy Spirit to encourage you when you are discouraged, and construct you when you feel self-destructive. There are times when you do not know what to pray for. Know that We are making intercession on your behalf. When you can utter a single word, your tears and groaning transmit messages to Us. We know what to do and will act suddenly.

Understand, My child, that I hear your petitions and requests. Make them know unto Me. Yes, I can read and know what is on your mind. I work those things out that you keep silent about; your heart-cry reveals them. Nevertheless, there are times when I want you to be mature enough to ask Me to do the hardest of things. I am able to intercede on your behalf. Your groans, moans, and pains have a language that I understand. Get ready for the healing power to overtake you in a new way today and you will feel super-charged by the Holy Spirit.

SCRIPTURES
Leviticus 26:8; 1 Corinthians 1:27, 15:25; Hebrews 7:25

HEALING PRAYER

Father, there is nothing like You standing in the gap for me. You are a fire wall of protection. Remove the smoke screens from my life and permit me access to revelation and clarity of my destiny and purpose. In Jesus' name, amen.

HEALING CONFESSIONS AND COMMANDS ACTIVATION

I CONFESS that God is making intercession for me and I am sitting with Him in heavenly places.

I CONFESS that the Father is working everything out on my behalf and I am not lacking what I have prayed unto the Father for.

I CONFESS AND COMMAND that my prayers are being heard by the Father and my prayers are coming to pass suddenly.

I CONFESS that God is Jehovah-Rophe—the God who heals me and He has taken my sickness and disease away from me.

I CONFESS AND COMMAND that I am not associated with people who don't believe in the healing power of God.

I CONFESS AND COMMAND that sickness and disease is not of God and Jesus has come to the earth to dismantle the works of evil.

I CONFESS AND COMMAND that my body is blessed and my body is the temple of the Holy Spirit, which is renewed daily like an eagle.

1 CORINTHIANS 3:16-17 (NIV)

*Don't you know that you yourselves are God's temple and
that God's Spirit lives in your midst? If anyone destroys
God's temple, God will destroy that person; for God's
temple is sacred, and you together are that temple.*

God's Sanctuary in You Should Be Holy

You are not an abandoned house or condemned place that cannot be restored and rebuilt. I remove the shame and blame of life that comes to defame and desecrate you. You are Mine and only Mine. For the enemy will attempt to close doors and opportunities, but I have given you the keys to the house of David, and I will open doors that no man or demon can slam shut. I will close doors that no man or demon can sling open. It is the adversary's plan to evict you and bring you to nothing. I come to break His curse and plan and expose his plots. Yes, I know, My child, that the trauma and abuse has caused fear to come to haunt your peaceful place.

I come to bring healing to your mind, soul, and body. I arrest those violators and evil spirits that come to remind you of what you desire to let go and forget. Cast those things on Me and I will restore your wholeness, peace, and joy. Turn over your new lease and agreement to Me and I will invade it with new glory. Your house will be filled with My presence and peace. My place is sacred, holy, and pure. Cleanse your soul with the Word of God and allow it to wash away those evil germs of the flesh. I will bring you spiritual gloves and sanitizers that will kill all evil bacteria that wants to take occupancy.

SCRIPTURES

Isaiah 22:22; John 10:28-29; Mark 3:27; Ephesians 5:26

HEALING PRAYER

Clean this inner place of my soul, Father. I want Your healing love to live there. Dwell in every dark place so that it will feel like a home and not a house. In Jesus' name, amen.

HEALING CONFESSIONS AND COMMANDS ACTIVATION

I CONFESS that I am God's sanctuary of healing and His holy temple.

I CONFESS that, in Jesus' name, I curse at the root every sickness, symptom, disease, pain, virus, discomfort, and infirmity that tries to attack my body or ever will.

I CONFESS AND COMMAND that I will eat healthy so that I will not aid disease, sickness, or immune deficiency.

I CONFESS AND COMMAND that sickness and disease have to hear me and obey me to leave.

I CONFESS AND COMMAND that I am whole and in sound mind and my body is renewed, healthy, purified by God's Word, revitalized, restored, strengthened, exercised, power-packed, strong, and built to overcome sickness and disease.

I CONFESS AND COMMAND that I will be happy and think on things that are healthy and blessed.

I CONFESS AND COMMAND that my body will not accept anything foreign or unhealthy, in Jesus' name.

I CONFESS AND COMMAND that sickness and disease will obey me as a citizen of Christ's Kingdom.

1 CORINTHIANS 12:7-10 (NIV)

Now to each one the manifestation of the Spirit is given for the common good. To one there is given through the Spirit a message of wisdom, to another a message of knowledge by means of the same Spirit, to another faith by the same Spirit, to another gifts of healing by that one Spirit, to another miraculous powers, to another prophecy, to another distinguishing between spirits, to another speaking in different kinds of tongues, and to still another the interpretation of tongues

God's Supernatural Gifts

I am uncapping your spiritual gifts that are within you today. Unlock and unload the power of the Holy Spirit that is ready to be released. You are much ahead that is in need of what you offer within you. Healing, miracles, personal prophetic words, and faith that are given to build, encourage, bless, edify, and assist others on their spiritual walk with Christ. These supernatural powers are not given by merit or by earnings, but given to those at birth. You are more than natural; you are made to be super-natural.

I want to stir up the gifts of the Spirit inside you and cause you to fan the flames. It will take your faith and My Spirit to spark a personal revival that will create a wildfire of mass revival to bring people unto Christ. Know, My child, that these special tools that I have imbedded in you will bring Me glory. I want to release more to those who are hungry and thirsty to be used more by Christ. You have been anointed for your generation. Arise and be that chain breaker!

SCRIPTURES
2 Timothy 1:16; 1 Corinthians 12:1

HEALING PRAYER

Father, active the gifts of healing that I may heal others with particular health or physical proclivities. Activate the gift of working of miracles to cure various diseases and the gift of prophecy to edify, encourage, and exhort the believer. In Jesus' name, amen.

HEALING CONFESSIONS AND COMMANDS ACTIVATION

I CONFESS that God's supernatural gifts in my life are presents for those who are Spirit-filled and saved.

I CONFESS that God is unlocking gifts in me for His glory to help others in His body.

I CONFESS that I will not be ignorant of spiritual gifts.

I CONFESS AND COMMAND that healing and divine healing and health fills me, surrounds me, keeps me, preserves me, and purifies my entire body and system.

I CONFESS that I will walk in faith that is required to bring about healing and miracles to others by the Holy Spirit.

I CONFESS AND COMMAND that I am loosed and free from any infirmity and sickness forever.

I CONFESS AND COMMAND that my health will spring up like the sun and diseases are removed and cured by the power of God.

I CONFESS AND COMMAND that sickness and disease will not take up residence in my temple where the Holy Spirit lives.

I CONFESS AND COMMAND that spiritual and natural toxins are being removed from out of my blood stream, arteries, values, system, bones, and body now, in Jesus' name.

2 CORINTHIANS 10:4-5 (NIV)

The weapons we fight with are not the weapons of the world. On the contrary, they have divine power to demolish strongholds. We demolish arguments and every pretension that sets itself up against the knowledge of God, and we take captive every thought to make it obedient to Christ.

God Demolishes Strongholds

Good morning, My warrior! As Captain of the God's Armies of Angels, I want you to know that there is a war going on in the spiritual realm. This war is a sour war and spiritual war over your purpose and destiny. The enemy had set up encampment around about you to wall you in. My spiritual intelligence and data does not malfunction or fail. From Heaven's headquarters, I send forth missile fires of destruction into the enemy's camp. I will bring down their strongholds and pillars erected in your life. I will demolish and penetrate its forces with My mighty hand.

Know that I am sending you spiritual information and intelligence to inform you that the weapons aimed at you are not natural weapons. They are spiritual machinery and artillery. You must fight spiritually, not carnally or by natural means. There are strongholds demonically set up against the knowledge of Me and they are contending against your faith in Christ. I will arm you with the divine power of the Holy Spirit to demolish these demonic boot camps in the spirit and have victory on every side.

SCRIPTURES

Joshua 5:14; Ephesians 6:12

HEALING PRAYER

Father, give me the Joshua grace and anointing to march around the walls of my spiritual Jericho and cause the walls to fall flat in my life for good. Give me the city that you can occupy for Your glory. In Jesus' name, amen.

HEALING CONFESSIONS AND COMMANDS ACTIVATION

I CONFESS that God's power demolishes demonic strongholds.

I CONFESS that God is changing my spiritual perspective daily and I am coming into the truth.

I CONFESS that the angels of the Lord are assigned to help me in my Christian walk.

I CONFESS AND COMMAND that the enemy may come in like a flood, but God will lift up a standard against him on my behalf.

I CONFESS AND COMMAND that I am exposed to the truth in God's Word as I read about the many miracles and healings that Jesus performed in His ministry on earth.

I CONFESS that God blesses my bread and water and all my food and drink.

I CONFESS AND COMMAND that I will not suffer from food poisoning, stomach virus, or any food allergies.

I CONFESS AND COMMAND that I walk in the divine will and purpose of God for my life daily.

I CONFESS that Jesus is the High Priest and Apostle of my confession.

I CONFESS AND COMMAND that the work of satan is destroyed, in Jesus' name.

2 Corinthians 12:9-10 (NIV)

But he said to me, "My grace is sufficient for you, for my power is made perfect in weakness." Therefore I will boast all the more gladly about my weaknesses, so that Christ's power may rest on me. That is why, for Christ's sake, I delight in weaknesses, in insults, in hardships, in persecutions, in difficulties. For when I am weak, then I am strong.

God Gives Enduring Grace to the Weak

Do not recall the horror of the past to be a present reality. The enemy wants control of your mind, will, and your emotions. He wants to recall the negative things to outweigh the positive things. Whether you encountered or faced sexual, verbal, physical, mental, or domestic abuse, I come to remove the sting and the poison that has left you numb. I will restore your innocence and peace. I will restore your love. It is my desire to keep you strong enough to put those things of the past behind you for the last time. The enemy calls as a serpent, as cunning as he can be, to whisper deception and lies that serve no positive outcome.

But know, My beloved, that I will not allow him to take advantage of what has already been done and seize on the moment. I will rescue you from the high waters and give you grace to stand on your two feet. My grace is sufficient when you are the insufficient. I will perfect those things concerning your life and smooth out the mountain cliffs that try to define you. You are a strong rock who cannot be moved, and this Rock is your anchor when you are sailing alone on life's ocean waters. Hardship, not shipwreck, will make you stronger while you are weak.

SCRIPTURES

Psalm 18:2; Isaiah 40:4, 45:2; Luke 3:5; 2 Corinthians 12:9

HEALING PRAYER

Father, Your enduring grace does not run out or dry up. It sustains me when I am depleted. You restore my strength when I am nauseous in the spirit. In Jesus' name, amen.

HEALING CONFESSIONS AND COMMANDS ACTIVATION

I CONFESS AND COMMAND that there is great grace extended to me by the Holy Spirit.

I CONFESS AND COMMAND that I will connect to a church, ministries, and Christians who believe the Word of God and the power of the Holy Spirit.

I CONFESS AND COMMAND that I believe in spiritual tongues, modern-day prophets, and apostles, miracles, healing, and deliverance.

I CONFESS AND COMMAND that the same Spirit who raised my Savior Jesus from the dead, quickens my mortal body every day, 24 hours, seven days a week.

I CONFESS AND COMMAND that I believe that I am healed and possess the miracle of God for my life.

I CONFESS that God receives glory to His name by the healing that I receive by faith.

I CONFESS AND COMMAND that every prophetic promise spoken over my life is yes and not denied as I walk in total obedience to God's Word.

I CONFESS AND COMMAND that my faith increases when **I CONFESS** the word of healing over my life daily.

EPHESIANS 2:19-22 (NIV)

Consequently, you are no longer foreigners and strangers, but fellow citizens with God's people and also members of his household, built on the foundation of the apostles and prophets, with Christ Jesus himself as the chief cornerstone. In him the whole building is joined together and rises to become a holy temple in the Lord. And in him you too are being built together to become a dwelling in which God lives by his Spirit.

God Is a Strong Foundation

You are not a stranger, My beloved one. You are My child and My heart jumps for joy over you. When I see you, I see Me, which is a reflection of My uniqueness in and through you. I created you fearfully and wonderfully Godlike in essence. You carry My DNA and through a regenerated spirit, you have now have been adopted into My household. You are being built on the foundation of Christ. You are being built upon His revelation knowledge, wisdom, and understanding of who He is daily in your life. There are works to do in My Kingdom, and you have an important part and role to play.

Like a movie, I am the Director and you are My main actor. As I sit on the throne of My Director's chair, the monologue of this movie script is your life's blueprint to walk out and fulfill. My Spirit dwelling in you will lead you and help you captivate your audience and win them for Christ in your generation. You are a leading actor who will receive the award and crown of life when the movie of your life ends. You are a healing model and voice of hope that people will see; your life is not just a movie but a lovely novel of your foundational relationship with Christ. The end of the earthly movie will be the beginning of a new blockbuster movie in Heaven.

SCRIPTURES

Romans 8:5,16; John 14:2

HEALING PRAYER

Thank You for being my strong foundation and causing me to have balance when I have fallen. In Jesus' name, amen.

HEALING CONFESSIONS AND COMMANDS ACTIVATION

I CONFESS that Jesus is my strong foundation and my healing is grounded in Him.

I CONFESS AND COMMAND that as I pray for God to heal me, I shall be healed; and when I cry out for salvation, He will save me as well (Jeremiah 17:14).

I CONFESS that Jesus is my Rock and my sure foundation daily that I can build upon.

I CONFESS AND COMMAND that as I return to the Lord each day, His presence brings healing, comfort, strength, and joy.

I CONFESS that God heal our backsliding and love us freely, for His anger has turned away from us (Hosea 14:4).

I CONFESS AND COMMAND that my spiritual house is built on the Word of God and it will not be torn down.

I CONFESS that as I fear the Lord, the Sun of Righteousness shall arise with healing in His wings; and I shall go out and frolic like well-fed calves (Malachi 4:2 NIV).

EPHESIANS 4:26-27 (NIV)

*In your anger do not sin: Do not let the sun go down while
you are still angry, and do not give the devil a foothold.*

God Releases Compassion to Forgive

It OK to be angry and passionate about something you believe in or disagree with. Passion and anger are feelings. I Myself get angry, upset, and disappointed at times when something isn't done as I have asked and directed for My children to do. In My anger, I do not make hasty decisions or emotional decisions that I will regret. I am a wise and loving God and Father. I am love and I possess real compassion. It is the same love that sent My Son to the earth to redeem humanity to Me. As you may be angry at times with others or even yourself, My child, think before you react. Exercise your faith and use wisdom when making decisions.

Your decisions today will be what you will live with tomorrow. Make sure it is the wisest decision, guided by the Holy Spirit. Learn to forgive others and yourself. In your anger, do not let sin be the foothold. Release anger and forgive others so that healing and deliverance will be your portion. Address anything that needs to be addressed as soon as possible, as a mature Christian believer. Do not let your good be evil spoken of. Yes, I know, My child, that you are not perfect. I did not make you perfect; yet I made you in My likeness to perfect those things concerning you. You hold the key to your destination as we together follow through on your purpose.

SCRIPTURES

Psalm 138:8; Matthew 10:16; Ephesians 4:26; Romans 14:16

HEALING PRAYER

Give me more compassion to love my enemies. Give me the boldness to settle any disputes as soon as they arise. In Jesus' name, amen.

HEALING CONFESSIONS AND COMMANDS ACTIVATION

I CONFESS that God releases compassion to those who ask Him to heal and forgive them.

I CONFESS AND COMMAND that my sins are forgiven and that **I CONFESS** my faults to others for personal freedom.

I CONFESS that God will continue to show mercy upon me daily and have compassion to heal me if I need it.

I CONFESS that I will not suffer from what the Lord Jesus has already suffered for on the cross for me.

I CONFESS that I am open to receive the love of God that permeates my heart to love Him even more.

I CONFESS AND COMMAND that when I cry out to the Lord to heal me, He does it and He will deliver my soul up from the grave and keep me alive; that I will not go down to the pit.

I CONFESS AND COMMAND that early and premature death is not my portion and I will live to fulfill my purpose and destiny.

EPHESIANS 5:15-18 (NIV)

Be very careful, then, how you live not as unwise but as wise, making the most of every opportunity, because the days are evil. Therefore do not be foolish, but understand what the Lord's will is. Do not get drunk on wine, which leads to debauchery. Instead, be filled with the Spirit....

God's Holy Spirit Outpouring

Be sober and vigilant in your Christian walk. You are not of the world who can be drunken with nature's wine; I want to pour out My Spirit upon all flesh so your sons and daughters will speak as oracles of Me. I will release the wisdom from Heaven to earth so that you know how to conduct yourself with integrity, morally and ethically. There is a Kingdom standard and way that I have established in My Word. Don't be conformed to the systems of this world. Walk in the Spirit and fulfill the desires of My heart. My child, days are becoming wicked and gross darkness has come upon the earth.

Know that you will be the light of the world through Christ who will shine and expose the enemy for what he really is—a defeated foe. I am pouring out My Holy Spirit in a new and unique way. As I did on the Day of Pentecost in the Upper Room, so shall it be in your day and generation. I am the God of the new. I am raising up new vessels of honor that will colonize the earth with My glory and presence. I desire to come down and live among My people as I did in the days of old. It may sound unrealistic, but that is a limited mentality and not faith. Believe what I am willing to do in your generation.

SCRIPTURES

Deuteronomy 5:33; Exodus 25:40; Joel 2:28-
29; 1 Corinthians 1:24; Acts 2:17

HEALING PRAYER

Pour out Your fresh wine and blow Your fresh wind upon me, Father. Release the Holy Spirit power that brings about change, healing, miracles, and blessing from on high. In Jesus' name, amen.

HEALING CONFESSIONS AND COMMANDS ACTIVATION

I CONFESS that the prophetic Spirit of God is pouring out upon me in a new way.

I CONFESS AND COMMAND that creativity, innovation, and originality is my portion, and I will live to see my dreams come to pass.

I CONFESS AND COMMAND that personal revival is being sparked by a passion for God like never before in my heart.

I CONFESS AND COMMAND that there will be mass revival and healing crusades that will ignite again in my city, community, church, ministry, region, and nation.

I CONFESS that the fresh baptism of the Holy Spirit will awaken a generation to operate in signs, wonders, and miracles.

I CONFESS AND COMMAND that I will be used greatly of the Lord for my generation to witness the raw power of God.

I CONFESS that my times and future are in the hands of God and that am presently walking out the promises of God for my life.

PHILIPPIANS 4:4-7 (NIV)

Rejoice in the Lord always. I will say it again: Rejoice! Let your gentleness be evident to all. The Lord is near. Do not be anxious about anything, but in everything, by prayer and petition, with thanksgiving, present your requests to God. And the peace of God, which transcends all understanding, will guard your hearts and your minds in Christ Jesus.

God Rejoices Over Those Who Rejoice

Rejoice in Me always, My loved one. I am not a Father who is far off looking; I am always near to those who call upon Me. When you are in trouble, I am present to deliver you. When you are in need of a financial bailout, I come to settle and pay off the invoice. Do not give the spirit of worry too much credit or the enemy the power to be a cosigner when your spiritual credit is not there. I am your Cosigner and I will ratify your spiritual financial conditions and give you a solution and action plan that will work. Together we will be liberated from the stress that comes with debt.

Praise Me in advance for what you are waiting on Me to release for you. There are things in your life that do not need a miracle but a plan. Let us create a freedom plan that will relieve any unnecessary stress that you have placed on yourself. Let us get rid of things that serve no value or purpose in your life. Through prayer and supplication, your request is being heard as you thank Me for following through. I want to settle your worries and give you peace that will surpass all understanding and guard your heart and mind that are secure in Christ.

SCRIPTURES

Ezekiel 20 (The Message); Zephaniah 3:17; Philippians 4:6

HEALING PRAYER

Father, I will rejoice in the face of personal opposition. I will not give the enemy credit for my personal victories. You rejoice over me and I am pleased. In Jesus' name, amen.

HEALING CONFESSIONS AND COMMANDS ACTIVATION

I CONFESS that God will rejoice over me with gladness.

I CONFESS AND COMMAND that many are the afflictions of the righteous, but the Lord will deliver me out of them all (Psalm 34:19).

I CONFESS that the Lord's light will break forth like the morning, and my healing shall spring forth speedily and I will not stay bound by what the enemy desires to put on me (Jeremiah 33:6).

I CONFESS AND COMMAND that I am a winner and not a loser and I shall defeat the odds that are against me.

I CONFESS AND COMMAND that every opposition and resistance is broken by the penetrating power of God.

I CONFESS AND COMMAND that I will be wise as a serpent and gentle as a dove.

I CONFESS AND COMMAND that I will not suffer from any hypertension, stroke, aneurism, or depression, in Jesus' name.

I CONFESS AND COMMAND that I shall be blessed all the days of my life and I will live in honor of His glory.

PHILIPPIANS 4:12-13 (NKJV)
I can do all things through Christ who strengthens me.

God Empowers You to Finish Strong

ood morning, My child, are you ready to start your day? I want to prepare your mind and body for a challenging day ahead. Even though you are faced with curve-ball situations, My dear one, you will be focused enough to hit those balls straight out of the park of your life. I will empower you with My Holy Spirit to soothe those tight areas in your life. Let Me stretch them out for you so that you are loose from them. With any great race, there must be great preparation. You must receive your morning nutrition that will give you the boost and the protein necessary to endure rigorous pressure. Understand that you will not get burned out nor will you feel drained. I will give you the inspiration needed to thrust you forward. You have to warm up first before you can finish your daily race.

Let's together rehearse being still in My presence and knowing that I am God. My dear child, rest in My arms as I massage and iron out the kinks in your life. The enemy wants you to pull a muscle, sprain a muscle, or even break a bone. However, I say not so, you will receive the calcium of My Word. For strong meat is for the mature. Having breakfast with Me prepares you for a winning race. You cannot win a race if you are injured, damaged, broken, tired, mentally defeated, or spiritually drained. I come to equip you by My Holy Spirit to give you the wings and winds behind you for a soaring victory each day.

SCRIPTURES
Isaiah 52:12, 58:8; Ecclesiastes 9:11

HEALING PRAYER

I will not settle for being last. Father, You have called me to be first and not last. Honor me with life's medal of honor of dedication to You as I obey You each and every day. In Jesus' name, amen.

HEALING CONFESSIONS AND COMMANDS ACTIVATION

I CONFESS AND COMMAND that I shall finish strong in everything that I have started and do for Christ.

I CONFESS AND COMMAND that I possess the finisher's anointing to accomplish the will of God for my life daily.

I CONFESS that the Holy Spirit of God has empowered me and equipped me to finish the work that the Father has sent me to the earth to do.

I CONFESS AND COMMAND that my meat and nourishment is to do the will of the Father like Jesus did when He walked the earth.

I CONFESS AND COMMAND that fasting and prayer will get rid of and break the ungodly, stubborn spirits and appetites.

I CONFESS that that God sent His Word and it has rescued me.

I CONFESS that God has made a way of escape for me when I am in trouble.

I CONFESS that the angels of the Lord protect me.

COLOSSIANS 2:8 (NIV)

See to it that no one takes you captive through hollow and deceptive philosophy, which depends on human tradition and the elemental spiritual forces of this world rather than on Christ.

God Breaks Worldly Deception and Methods

*M*y child, hear My voice today as I want to liberate any thoughts that come from the world. You are not a robot or made a carbon copy of something already created. You must understand that when I created you, you were purposed to be very different in appearance. Even if you are a twin, there is a distinction and unique fingerprint. I have done this on purpose that every single human being is not a duplicate but the original I have created him or her to be. You also were not created from a monkey or any evolution theory—in the beginning you were in Me and everything was created by Me. I come to break every deception and philosophy that brings about a different perspective of Me.

I break you free from any gospel that denies the life, ministry, work, death, burial, and resurrection of My Beloved Son, Jesus. I want to break you free from all doctrines and teachings of men that do not believe in the work of the Holy Spirit, gifts of the Spirits, or ministry gifts given to the church, that of modern-day apostles and prophets, tongues, gift of prophecy, and the supernatural. I am the God who gives theses remarkable gifts to the church as foundational ministries and gifts by the Holy Spirit to bring truth of Christ and to build the Church corporately.

SCRIPTURES

Matthew 7:15-20; 2 Corinthians 10:5;
Galatians 1:8; Ephesians 2:20

HEALING PRAYER

Father, break every pattern and system of worldliness in my life. I want to be liberated by the Holy Spirit and walk in the power of the Spirit. In Jesus' name, amen.

HEALING CONFESSIONS AND COMMANDS ACTIVATION

I CONFESS AND COMMAND that magic, witchcraft, and false miracles have no place in my life and break its power, in Jesus' name.

I CONFESS AND COMMAND that tricks, gimmicks, and charismatic witchcraft is not the nature of God and has no authority over me, in Jesus' name.

I CONFESS AND COMMAND that the wisdom of men is not what I operate in; I operate in the wisdom and counsel of the Lord.

I CONFESS that God comforts me when I am discomforted.

I CONFESS AND COMMAND that I shall not be deceived by worldly deception, man-made methods, legalism, or deceptive philosophies.

I CONFESS that I am a God-fearing believer and I am radical for Jesus.

I CONFESS AND COMMAND that my mind, body, and soul is in agreement with the will of God and shall function to its full capacity daily.

I COMMAND that nothing in my sphere of influence will be poisoned by ungodly toxins or plagues by the enemy.

COLOSSIANS 3:12-14 (NIV)

Therefore, as God's chosen people, holy and dearly loved, clothe yourselves with compassion, kindness, humility, gentleness and patience. Bear with each other and forgive one another if any of you has a grievance against someone. Forgive as the Lord forgave you. And over all these virtues put on love, which binds them all together in perfect unity.

God Heals, Forgives, and Liberates

I have chosen you as a special candidate for healing and miracles. You will be used, My child, to raise the standard of righteous living. People will admire you and want to follow you because you follow Christ. What an awesome opportunity it will be for you to be a prophetic voice of change for this generation. You will be a spiritual advocate for those who have experienced injustice in one way or another. Through the Holy Spirit, you will have the ability to pardon and forgive people of their wrongdoings, just as I am quick to forgive you of yours. My child, I will mantle you with a robe of humility, compassion, kindness, gentleness, and patience.

People will come to you in need of advice to make the right decision, and you will lead them to Me while offering them spiritual wisdom by My Word that will free them, heal them, bless them, help them, and relieve them. You will be marked with love that will be noticed. As you hear people's issues, pains, and problems, the Holy Spirit in you will stir you up and give you the spontaneous answer to give them. It will surprise you at first; but as you come in concert with the Holy Spirit's leading and voice, you will grow familiar with My constant voice daily. I desire to see total victory, forgiveness, and liberation in those who are sick, bound, victimized, and oppressed.

SCRIPTURES

Isaiah 55:7; John 15:16; Romans 8:14

HEALING PRAYER

Father, allow me to be a conduit of forgiveness. Never allow me to harbor any resentment in my heart. Shine light on it so that I will be free and healed totally. In Jesus' name, amen.

HEALING CONFESSIONS AND COMMANDS ACTIVATION

I CONFESS AND COMMAND that God has healed me, liberated me, and forgives me for all my wrongdoings.

I CONFESS AND COMMAND that will not walk in partial healing but total healing in my mind, body, and soul.

I CONFESS AND COMMAND that unforgiveness will not hinder nor close Heaven over my life.

I CONFESS AND COMMAND that unforgiveness will not cause me to miss Heaven and the promises of God for my life.

I CONFESS AND COMMAND that when I pray for healing, deliverance, and for a miracle, that it is mine.

I CONFESS that I will possess the spiritual armor of God and I will stand in faith against the wiles and devices of the devil (Ephesians 6:11; 2 Corinthians 2:11).

I CONFESS AND COMMAND that I will stand, having done all to stand, until I see the physical manifestation of my healing, deliverance, and miracle (Ephesians 6:13).

I CONFESS AND COMMAND that healing is what I desire each day and it is working in me now, in Jesus' name.

HEBREWS 1:14 (NIV)
Are not all angels ministering spirits sent to
serve those who will inherit salvation?

God Sends Ministering Angels

*Y*ou are a joint heir of My eternal Kingdom. When you gave your life over to Jesus, My Son, you were made an heir of this marvelous Kingdom. As a result of your earnest decision, I have assigned you as one of those who will inherit salvation and this Kingdom. For it is My desire to give you the Kingdom. I have sent ministering angels to those who will receive salvation. When you are hungry after fasting, I will send angel food by the Spirit to give you strength for the journey. Your purpose and assignment in the earth is so great that even the devil has sent demon spirits to oppose you. For that very fact, I have counteracted his divisive plan with warring angels and ministering spirits to help you fulfill your God-given calling uninterrupted.

Sickness, disease, poverty, and trauma will not hold you hostage. I will break you free and heal any emotional damage that life has done in the process. There are things that you may have encountered that are too much to bear and endure. It was unbelievable when it happened to you. Nevertheless, believe Me that I can erase the pain and bad memories. You will walk in regret, but you will forget those things behind you and press toward the mark, reaching toward the high calling that is in Christ Jesus. Pray that I will send ministering angels to guard you and strengthen you in times of need.

SCRIPTURES
Psalm 78:25; Romans 8:17; Hebrews 1:14, 8:12

HEALING PRAYER

Send Your ministering spirits to me when I am weak. Give me angel food that will nourish me as I read, study, and meditate upon Your Word, Father. In Jesus' name, amen.

HEALING CONFESSIONS AND COMMANDS ACTIVATION

I CONFESS that God's ministering angels are feeding me what I need to strengthen me.

I CONFESS that God has sent His angels to give charge over me.

I CONFESS AND COMMAND that when I am weak the angels of the Lord are there to serve as spiritual nurses to monitor my progress.

I CONFESS that I am submitting to God's Word daily for me to see and receive the benefits of what His Word says I can obtain.

I CONFESS AND COMMAND that whatever I decree today by faith I will walk in tomorrow.

I CONFESS AND COMMAND I am actively fighting against all sickness with the help of angelic reinforcement (1 Peter 5:8-9).

I CONFESS AND COMMAND that I will fight the good fight of faith and when my faith is tested, my endurance has a chance to grow (James 1:3).

I CONFESS AND COMMAND that my lifestyle is not contrary to the will of God.

I CONFESS AND COMMAND that healing is my heavenly portion.

I CONFESS AND COMMAND that I will not be in this condition for the rest of my life, in Jesus' name.

JAMES 4:7 (NIV)
Submit yourselves, then, to God. Resist the
devil, and he will flee from you.

God Goes Before You in War

*S*ubmit daily to My leading, My beloved one. Each day I have new things to unfold to you. I desire for you to tap into your spiritual creativity to bring forth these new things. Do not get bottled down by what seems to be working in the world system. Those things have an unfortunate ending. I have a promising ending, which is really the beginning for those whom I call Mine. As you comply to the Holy Spirit's leading, you will gain a greater understanding of what I have already worked out for you. I will not deceive you. Take My hand and allow Me to walk you through the valley of death. You will fear no evil for knowing with assurance that your hand is in My hand. I have gone before you and saw the enemy's plan—and the way of escape.

The enemy will not see you coming; you will catch him off course even when he tries to catch you slipping. Know, My child, that I have your footing and you will not slip or fall on the ice rink of life. I will skate with you, and together we will become a great partnership to success. I have given you authority and graced you with power to resist the enemy of your purpose and he will run from you. The devil only recognizes authentic authority. Give voice to that which I have placed within you. Tell sickness to flee today, disease to flee today, poverty to flee today, demon spirits to flee today.

SCRIPTURES

Deuteronomy 30:9; James 4:7; Luke 10:19; 3 John 1:2

HEALING PRAYER

Father, You are the Lord of the breakthrough. You break through every enemy defense against me. Give me more to look forward to each day. In Jesus' name, amen.

HEALING CONFESSIONS AND COMMANDS ACTIVATION

I CONFESS that if God is before me, then who can be against me? Knowing this truth, I will not walk in the spirit of fear.

I CONFESS that God is the Captain of the God armies and there is more with me than against me.

I CONFESS AND COMMAND that I will not settle for less but pursue all that God has for me.

I CONFESS that I will keep my confidence and profession in God's Word regardless of what report I have received from the doctors (Ephesians 6:13).

I CONFESS that I will always consider Jesus Christ as the Apostle and High Priest of my confession daily (Hebrews 3:1).

I CONFESS AND COMMAND that I will not permit myself to get into a place of fear or an unbelief mentality (John 4:48).

I CONFESS AND COMMAND that if I hear a bad report or unfavorable second opinion that I will not fall into fear, but will tap into faith by God's Word (Luke 8:50).

I CONFESS AND COMMAND that I have a sanctified imagination and I have prophetic insight to my personal healing.

JAMES 5:14-15 (NIV)

*Is anyone among you sick? Let them call the elders of the church to
pray over them and anoint them with oil in the name of the Lord.
And the prayer offered in faith will make the sick person well; the
Lord will raise them up. If they have sinned, he will be forgiven.*

God Anoints Leadership with Healing Powers

I have given wisdom to those who desire to become doctors and surgeons. It
is my passion to break through in modern medicine and perform miracles
that will bring healing to those in need. Hospitals are places to help the sick
to recover, to provide attention to the hurt, injured, and bruised. Naturally, if
you are sick, My child, you would go to your primary physician; or if it's an
emergency, that you will take yourself to the emergency room to be cared for.

There is another place where most people do not think about going in
times of crisis and in need of medical attention. The church is another powerful entity and hub of miracles, healing, and deliverance where the Holy
Spirit can solve any physical and spiritual issue. Know that I have placed
within the church leadership, leaders who can pray for the sick people and
anoint them with oil—and in the name of Jesus, the sick are healed. There
is a prayer of faith offered in times when the sick are made whole. Even if the
sick have sinned, they also can be relieved and forgiven. I have made those

who are called to be doctors in the earth, but the church is an anointed place to receive healing and miracle breakthrough.

SCRIPTURES
Isaiah 53:5; John 5:1-9

HEALING PRAYER

When I am ill, Lord, I know where to go to receive prayers of faith to release the healing and miracle that I am standing in line for. Thanks for the truth in Your Word. In Jesus' name, amen.

HEALING CONFESSIONS AND COMMANDS ACTIVATION

I CONFESS AND COMMAND that I will connect to a Spirit-filled, covenant-keeping, and anointed leadership in the church who understand the miracles and ministry of Jesus.

I CONFESS AND COMMAND that my relationships are changing and they are healthy relationships, affiliations, associations, and partnerships that serve as a mutual benefit to advance the Kingdom of God.

I CONFESS AND COMMAND that I will be part of a sound Bible teaching church that understand the gifts of the Spirit and the operation of the Holy Spirit's power.

I CONFESS AND COMMAND that when my patience or endurance is fully developed, I will be mature and complete, not lacking anything (James 1:2-8).

I CONFESS AND COMMAND that I will not allow my mind to be conformed to this world system, but will renew my mind each day (Romans 12:2).

I CONFESS AND COMMAND that faith is now not a thing of the past but a personal confidence and hope in God and His Word (Hebrews 11:1,6).

I CONFESS that I will take into account and commit to memory that faith comes by hearing the Word of God—not by having heard the Word of God in the past. My faith now comes by hearing the *rhema* Word of God (Romans 10:17).

JAMES 5:16 (NIV)
Therefore confess your sins to each other and pray for
each other so that you may be healed. The prayer of
a righteous person is powerful and effective.

God Answers the Righteous in Faith

*D*id you know that confession is a great solution to apply in your deliverance? It is always the eviction of demons that will solve every oppressing and depressing issue; but it is a decision to be honest with yourself about what struggles, addictions, and strongholds to give up. You understand, My child, that confession is 90 percent of the deliverance that brings about freedom. Deliverance and casting out of demonic spirits and oppressing spirits has a whole different dynamic. I will not have you ignorant of the enemy's devices. Confess your faults one to another and free yourself from any snares that the enemy will set up as personal defeats.

Do not settle for anything; put your foot down, put it in the enemy's mouth and let him taste defeat (the feet). He will not snare you by your testimony; you will be free to confess your sins to another believer in Christ and pray the prayer of healing. Know that the prayer of a righteous person is powerful, effective, and responsive. I answer the prayers of the righteous in faith. Prayers for emotional, physical, mental, and spiritual healing by a believer releases the answer and healing. My child, you are a vehicle I will use to pray from earth and see answers released from Heaven simultaneously.

SCRIPTURES
Psalm 30:2; James 5:16; Romans 16:20

HEALING PRAYER

I know now that my prayers are not held up until my faith is released for them to be answered. Like Daniel who prayed and Father you answered his prayers, but they were held up in the heavens. Send warring angels to release my breakthrough now! In Jesus' name, amen.

HEALING CONFESSIONS AND COMMANDS ACTIVATION

I CONFESS AND COMMAND that I will speak the life-giving, spiritual word of Christ daily over my personal situation (John 6:63).

I CONFESS that God will answer me because I am His child.

I CONFESS that God acts on behalf of His people by faith who are in need of Him.

I CONFESS that Jesus declared that by my words I will be justified, and by my words I will be condemned.

I CONFESS AND COMMAND my mouth not to utter idle words, vain sayings, and words of ignorance, noneffective words from loose lips. I will use the Word of God with my mouth; my heart will overflow with faith and my mouth will speak faith (Matthew 12:34-37).

I CONFESS AND COMMAND that I will speak what I want to manifest prophetically by the Word of God (Mark 11:23).

I CONFESS AND COMMAND that I will only speak and say what I want to see manifest or come to pass, to become, to come into being or in existence, in Jesus' name (Mark 11:23).

I CONFESS AND COMMAND that I will not speak what I do not want to come to pass. I know that I have the same spirit of faith, according as it is written, I believed, and therefore have I spoken. I also believe, and therefore speak (Psalm 116:10; 2 Corinthians 4:13).

JOHN 11:38-44 (NIV)

Jesus, once more deeply moved, came to the tomb. It was a cave with a stone laid across the entrance. "Take away the stone," he said. "But, Lord," said Martha, the sister of the dead man, "by this time there is a bad odor, for he has been there four days." Then Jesus said, "Did I not tell you that if you believe, you will see the glory of God?" So they took away the stone. Then Jesus looked up and said, "Father, I thank you that you have heard me. I knew that you always hear me, but I said this for the benefit of the people standing here, that they may believe that you sent me." When he had said this, Jesus called in a loud voice, "Lazarus, come out!" The dead man came out, his hands and feet wrapped with strips of linen, and a cloth around his face. Jesus said to them, "Take off the grave clothes and let him go."

God Raises the Dead and Frees the Bound

Good morning, My friend. I want to assure you that whatever losses you have incurred in this season, know that I will give you more than enough and restore the times that have been disposed. I want to reveal to you My glory in a new way that you are not familiar with. Your faith, My child, will cause you to see the glory of Me. I can disclose levels of My glory in unusual ways that will cause mouths to open and eyes to stare in awe. There is no sickness, disease, issue, disability, demon spirit, or poverty that can stand in My way. Those temporal things may seem like boulders that are impossible to smash, defeat, and remove.

They are lightweight to Me. I will remove every stony place in your life. I will remove the caves of your soul and shine the light of My glory in. I will call forth every dead thing, situation, and circumstance and cause it to obey Me. I hold life in My mouth. I speak to earth, winds, heavens, and seasons, and they obey My voice. Know that I possess the power to unravel every blockage and free you today. Believe My Word and know that I am the Life. I will unbind the oppressed, heal the sick, raise anything that has died, and cure what is diseased. Know that I am in the wonder-working business.

SCRIPTURES

Isaiah 10:27; Psalm 55:22; Matthew 10:8

HEALING PRAYER

I am free by the Holy Spirit and I will not get bound up again. In Jesus' name, amen.

HEALING CONFESSIONS AND COMMANDS ACTIVATION

I CONFESS that God resurrects anything that has died in my life that wasn't supposed to die.

I CONFESS AND COMMAND that I am free from any stronghold that has kept me bound for some time.

I CONFESS AND COMMAND that I am freer today than I have ever been and sin will not keep me in bondage.

I CONFESS AND COMMAND that every python spirit and spirit of division is cut off and destroyed by the power of God.

I CONFESS AND COMMAND that the spirit of death will not follow me and I have abundant life in Christ.

I CONFESS AND COMMAND that every word curse sent to destroy me and fiery dart to assassinate me will fall and never rise again.

I CONFESS AND COMMAND that I will surround myself with believers when I need to do the impossible (Luke 8:51).

1 PETER 5:7 (NIV)

Cast all your anxiety on him because he cares for you.

God Relieves Stress, Worries, and Fears

I am concerned about your well-being, know that My Kingdom will provide the provision of spiritual assistance in times of need or crisis. I see what you face day-to-day and the responsibility that you carry to keep things together. You endure much and at times you are not recognized for all your efforts. It is my heart for you, My dear one, not to overwork yourself. Every burden is not a burden that I have given you. Some burdens can be sent to hinder you and slow you down from accomplishing what I have desired and purposed for you to do. The enemy wants you to wave the white flag to surrender your will to him. He also wants you to dedicate all of your time, money, resources, gifts, talents, and intelligence to things that are not in My will.

Those things can be underlining death traps overall. It is his intent to get you so stress out and walking in the spirit of anxiety that you will carry around with you worry and a heavy heart. This will trigger heart attacks, high blood pressure, and phobias that are unhealthy. I curse those assignments of the enemy. I regulate your blood, your sugar level, and your health. I detach you from any evil spirits and cares of this world. I place upon you My peace and My burden. I remove every false expectation given to you out of season and familiarity. I say, My chosen one, You will walk in liberty and receive what is rightfully yours in this season. My Word will not return unto Me void, and I will say that My love will not return unto Me empty but will establish a place in your heart. Get lost in My love regardless how you feel physically; My love will overshadow and trump it.

SCRIPTURES

Psalm 55:11; Matthew 23:4; 2 Corinthians 2:11; 1 John 4:8,16

HEALING PRAYER

Father, when I am stressed and frustrated. I know that I can run to You and I am safe. Remove the expectations of others and mantle my shoulders with only Your responsibilities. In Jesus' name, amen.

HEALING CONFESSIONS AND COMMANDS ACTIVATION

I CONFESS AND COMMAND that obedience is better than sacrifice and will do what God has designated me to do.

I CONFESS that the Lord will relieve all the pain, stress, and worries that have been placed on my shoulders.

I CONFESS AND COMMAND that I will be responsible over the charge and burden that God has given to me.

I CONFESS AND COMMAND that I am freeing myself from any burdens that are not in the purpose, plan, and will of God for my life.

I CONFESS AND COMMAND that stress and depression will not cause premature death, stroke, or illness by any means.

I CONFESS AND COMMAND that I will enjoy the Kingdom of God here and now on earth.

I CONFESS AND COMMAND that I will walk in humility before the Lord and He will exalt me in due season.

DAY 88

1 John 4:4 (NIV)

You, dear children, are from God and have overcome them, because
the one who is in you is greater than the one who is in the world.

God Works Wonders

*D*id you know that you were created for so much more? It is the intent of the devil to bring the fogs of life to distort your vision and ability to see ahead of you. When you get close enough to see, then it's too late. You are suddenly faced head-on with a deer or elk caught in your path. I come to remove the head-on collisions of life and absorb the impact. I will not permit you to be hijacked by distracted by objects that the enemy places in your way. Do not allow a bad doctor's report, a physical flaw or deformity, obesity, eating disorder, depression, oppression, disability, or poverty to limit you. Faith overcomes fear. I want to do a supernatural work in you and through you for My glory. I have prayer-proofed your life with the ability by the Holy Spirit to endure anything that comes your way.

You have the greatest opportunity to shine like the sun, to witness to the overcoming power of the Holy Spirit. The woman with the issue of blood for twelve years needed a miracle and she was exposed to Jesus by touching His garment. The virtues went out of Him and into her and dried up her lifelong issue. I want to do the same work in you that I did in My Son Jesus. I am willing and more than able to do great things in you. Are you ready to be a sign and a wonder to your generation? Receive the power today to fill yourself up.

251

SCRIPTURES
*Numbers 6:25; Matthew 10:22; Luke
8:43-48; 2 Timothy 3:12*

HEALING PRAYER

*I want to be used for Your purpose and glory on earth, Father. Place
me in an environment that is conducive for Your work to be released in
and through me. In Jesus' name, amen.*

HEALING CONFESSIONS AND
COMMANDS ACTIVATION

I CONFESS that God will work miracles, signs, and wonders through me
as I submit to the Holy Spirit's leading.

I CONFESS that greater is He in me than he that is in the world and God
will prove Himself strong in me daily.

I CONFESS that Jesus is my Refuge to whom I run and am secure.

I CONFESS and believe that miracles and healing is for today and God has
not stopped performing His mighty acts.

I CONFESS AND COMMAND that my life will be a testimony of the miraculous power of God through word and deed.

I CONFESS that I will have the God-like creative faith that frames my
world by the Word of God so that things that are seen are made of things
that do not appear; or things we now see did not come from anything that
can be seen (Hebrews 11:3).

I CONFESS and believe in my heart what the Scriptures state, that Jesus
received those who believe and spoke to them about the Kingdom of God,
and healed those in need of healing (Luke 9:11).

1 JOHN 4:18 (NIV)

*There is no fear in love. But perfect love drives out fear, because fear has
to do with punishment. The one who fears is not made perfect in love.*

God Imparts His Healing Love

I know that at times you have to do things on your own to make it. I want
you to trust Me and allow Me to work on your behalf. Take a deep breath
and render those things unto Me. I will care for you and provide for you.
Regardless what the situation may look like, I hold the key to the outcome.
My child, I want you to know that everything is working together for you. I
will put fear to shame through the supernatural faith that you will walk in
this season. This is a time when I am going to release the love that will shatter
all unwelcome fears and hurts. You have been through enough. You are free
from any old obligations by others and those you love.

I know it's hard to trust people; after all, people have a tendency to let us
down at the most critical moments of need. I know it's hard to love when
love is just a four-letter word to some people. I am the meaning of love, and I
am Love. Know today that there is no fear in love. It is perfect love that will
drive out all of your past and present fears. Fear will judge, but love will jus-
tify. The one who fears is not made perfect in love—the one who loves has
overcome fear. Receive My love that will heal every broken heart and will
become the stitch that will knit our hearts together.

SCRIPTURES
Psalm 34:18, 147:3; Romans 8:28

HEALING PRAYER

Your love toward me sheds light to Your intentions and truth of Your Word. Allow me to be earmarked with Your love that will compel others to You. In Jesus' name, amen.

HEALING CONFESSIONS AND COMMANDS ACTIVATION

I CONFESS that the love of Christ heals old and present wounds.

I CONFESS that the love of Christ covers and does not expose faults, errors, and sin.

I CONFESS that God will impart His healing love that will bring peace and comfort.

I CONFESS that there is no fear in love but perfect love drives out all fear in my life.

I CONFESS that the Scriptures states that if the prayer of faith is prayed, that the Lord shall raise me up (James 5:14).

I CONFESS AND COMMAND that I will continue to confess and profess divine healing by the Word of God and believe that I shall receive it by faith, until I see the physical manifestation of healing (Matthew 21:22).

I CONFESS AND COMMAND that my body, organs, tissues, bones, blood, and cells are made alive by the same power that raised up Jesus Christ from the dead.

1 JOHN 4:19 (NIV)

We love because he first loved us.

3 JOHN 2 (NIV)

Dear friend, I pray that you may enjoy good health and that all
may go well with you, even as your soul is getting along well.

God Performs Soul Surgery

My love for you extends beyond the expanse of the universe. It is an ever-lasting eternal love that cannot be separated. It is My heart's desire and joy to see you in great health and that all is well with you. I guard you daily to make sure of that. I am here to bring healing to your soul and settle any battles in your mind, will, and emotions. I can hear what is on your heart, witness your passions and inner-most desires, and understand your decisions. Know, My child, that I loved and chose you first. You did not choose Me, I handpicked you. I was delighted to know that you made an earnest decision and sacrifice to give up everything to follow Christ. That was one of the best, if not *the* best, decisions you could have ever made.

The enemy was let down once and for all because of your choice to love, serve, worship, and embrace Me and My Beloved Son, Jesus. It was the power of choice that I commend you and honor you for. It has always been the adversary's plan to get as many lost souls on his side. That wasn't the case for you. Because I have already put My bid in, and like Job, you made the con-science decision not to reject Me or curse me because of what you may have encountered throughout your life. I have come to mend the broken fences and rebuilt the waste places. I have come like a heart surgeon to perform soul surgery to every area that was previously and presently damaged. Know today that Heaven has declared your healing; and now, My child, walk in it with liberty in Christ. I love you!

SCRIPTURES

Job 2:9; John 3:16; Ephesians 3:19; Philippians 4:7; 1 John 4:8,16

HEALING PRAYER

Thank You, Father, for helping me overcome this season. I am ready to embark on a new one with victory and receive my total liberty, healing, personal deliverance, and blessings from Heaven. In Jesus' name, amen.

HEALING CONFESSIONS AND COMMANDS ACTIVATION

I CONFESS that Jesus continues to do soul surgery by His Word.

I CONFESS that Jesus sets me free from all infirmity because He has loosened and set me free from the bondage of satan (Luke 13:12,16).

I CONFESS AND COMMAND that I will not lack anything that God has promised me each day.

I CONFESS AND COMMAND that sin has no rule over me and satan can't hold me in bondage because I have been loosed from my infirmities by Jesus Christ (Luke 13:12).

I CONFESS AND COMMAND that unnecessary yokes and ungodly burdens have been unfastened, untied, destroyed, dissolved, declared unlawful, and deprived of authority in my life.

I CONFESS that the love of God will do heart surgery and bring total deliverance and healing to my heart.

I CONFESS AND COMMAND that I am in a great season of success and prosperity and healing.

I CONFESS AND COMMAND that I am in good health and will not permit any viral infection, bacteria, or virus to invade my life and body.

I CONFESS AND COMMAND that sickness, disease, and pain will never come back or any reoccurring problem, in Jesus' name.

About the Author

*D*r. Hakeem Collins is an empowerment specialist, respected emerging prophetic voice, governmental minister, life coach, and sought-after conference speaker. He is known for his keen, accurate prophetic gifting and supernatural ministry. He is the founder of Champions International, The Prophetic Academy, and Revolution Network based in Wilmington, Delaware, where he resides. He is the author of several books: *Heaven Declares* and *Prophetic Breakthrough*. He has been featured on many television, streaming, and radio programs including Sid Roth's *It's Supernatural* and *Cornerstone TV.*

MINISTRY CONTACT INFORMATION

Champions International
c/o Dr. Hakeem Collins
PO Box 305
Wilmington, DE 19899
Office Phone: 302-388-7558
bookingtwinprophets@gmail.com
info@hakeemcollinsministries.com
www.hakeemcollinsministries.com

SOCIAL MEDIA CONTACT INFORMATION

Facebook: www.facebook.com/drhakeemcollins
Instagram: www.instagram.com/drhakeemcollins
Twitter: www.twitter.com/hakeem_collins
Youtube: www.youtube.com/hakeemcollinstv

DONATE INFORMATION

www.hakeemcollinsministries.com/donate-2/
www.Paypal.me/hakeemcollins

Made in the USA
Lexington, KY
18 August 2019